"The let's-sit-down-and-chat-about-this style of this book is brilliant. David has done a superb job paralleling SLT with Bible narratives, then drawing on his experiences to give broad, practical advice in a short book, not dodging the issues, but highlighting good practices. This is an insightful, easy read that I would recommend to all involved in short-term teams."

—HOWARD AND AVE ROBINSON
Director, Mobile Mission Maintenance New Zealand

"This book wonderfully illustrates that mission trips are at their best when they incorporate service and learning! Dr. Entwistle offers very practical, down-to-earth advice that is applicable to individuals involved in many types of mission work, helping them to avoid common pitfalls by learning about the culture instead of judging it, listening to those who live on the field and following their recommendations, and approaching the trip with the heart of a servant. As missionaries who have hosted hundreds of teams over the past eighteen years, we appreciate how this book can help prepare people not just to go on a mission trip to help others, but to understand that they will also be transformed by the experience."

—ALLEN AND TRISH SOWERS
Missionaries to Honduras, Founders, Sowers4Pastors, Inc

"Having been with Dr. Entwistle and some of his teams, I can affirm that the wisdom imparted in this short treatise has sometimes been learned the hard way. He has seen lives and futures changed as young men and women have embarked on service-learning teams that impacted them as well as those in the host cultures. Insightful, practical, and challenging, the questions raised in this book are designed to make the most out of any cross-cultural experience. Like never before, the world awaits those who are willing to rise to the challenges, to embark on the journey, to see lives changed by exposure to others from other cultures. Great opportunities to learn and serve should begin with careful reading and discussion of this book."

—DON & BETTY ORR
Humanitarian aid workers

"Service-Learning Teams offer a tremendous opportunity for individuals and teams to grow personally and spiritually, while providing meaningful help to ongoing ministry. However, this growth and impact is only achieved when there is a strong biblical foundation of service and calling, along with guidance on navigating thorny issues like team conflict, finances, and cross-cultural sensitivity. Drawing on years of experience and keen biblical insight, Dr. Entwistle provides the tools necessary to help individuals and teams to think through the fundamental components of a short-term mission to maximize the personal and spiritual growth of participants and their effectiveness in ministry."

—PJ HOLMERTZ
International Short-Term Program Director, Africa Inland Mission

The Service Learning Book

The Service Learning Book

*Getting Ready, Serving Well,
and Coming Back Transformed*

DAVID N. ENTWISTLE

CASCADE *Books* • Eugene, Oregon

THE SERVICE LEARNING BOOK
Getting Ready, Serving Well, and Coming Back Transformed

Copyright © 2019 David N. Entwistle. All rights reserved. Except for brief quotations in critical publications or reviews, no part of this book may be reproduced in any manner without prior written permission from the publisher. Write: Permissions, Wipf and Stock Publishers, 199 W. 8th Ave., Suite 3, Eugene, OR 97401.

Cascade Books
An Imprint of Wipf and Stock Publishers
199 W. 8th Ave., Suite 3
Eugene, OR 97401

www.wipfandstock.com

PAPERBACK ISBN: 978-1-5326-7486-0
HARDCOVER ISBN: 978-1-5326-7487-7
EBOOK ISBN: 978-1-5326-7488-4

Cataloguing-in-Publication data:

Entwistle, David N. (David Nelson), author.

The service learning book: getting ready, serving well, and coming back transformed / David N. Entwistle.

Description: Eugene, OR: Cascade Books, 2019. | Includes bibliographical references.

Identifiers: ISBN 978-1-5326-7486-0 (paperback). | ISBN 978-1-5326-7487-7 (hardcover). | ISBN 978-1-5326-7488-4 (ebook).

Subjects: LCSH: Service learning. | Education, Higher—Aims and objectives—United States. | Community and college. | Short-term missions. | Cultural intelligence.

Classification: LC220.5 E66 2019 (paperback). | LC220.5 (ebook).

Manufactured in the U.S.A.   07/26/19

Dedicated to Don and Betty Orr, and those like them
who serve Christ and the church far from their homes, and to
Daniel, Gosia, Tymek, Julia, Martyna, and Jeremi Masarczyk
who have become my second family.

Pragnę cię zobaczyć. Nie mogę zapomnieć twoich łez.
Tęsknię więc za radością spotkania z tobą.

"In the twilight of life, God will not judge us on our earthly possessions and human successes, but on how well we have loved."

—Saint John of the Cross

And the end of all our exploring
Will be to arrive where we started
And know the place for the first time.

—T. S. Eliot
"Little Gidding"

Contents

Permissions | ix
Preface | xi
Acknowledgments | xiii

1 What's It All About? Service Learning Overview | 1
2 Should I Go? Billboards, Nudges, and Wisdom | 7
3 Second Thoughts and Cold Feet | 21
4 Let's Talk about Money | 32
5 Blessings and Trials of Being a Traveling Companion | 48
6 Increasing Your Cross-Cultural Competency | 57
7 Packing Lists—Don't Forget Your Passport! | 71
8 Whatever You Do . . . | 81
9 Reflections during Service Learning Experiences | 91
10 Finishing Well | 101
11 Looking Back | 108

Bibliography | 115
Additional Resources | 117

Permissions

Scripture marked (NIV) are taken from the Holy Bible, NEW INTERNATIONAL VERSION®, NIV® Copyright © 1973, 1978, 1984, 2011 by Biblica, Inc.® Used by permission. All rights reserved worldwide.

Scripture quotations marked (CEB) are taken from Common English Bible® Copyright © 2010, 2011 by Common English Bible,™ Used by permission. All rights reserved worldwide

Scripture quotations marked (NLT) are taken from The Holy Bible, New Living Translation, copyright © 1996, 2004, 2015 by Tyndale House Foundation. Used by permission of Tyndale House Publishers, Inc., Carol Stream, Illinois 60188. All rights reserved.

Scripture quotations marked (ICB) are taken from the International Children's Bible®. Copyright © 1986, 1988, 1999 by Thomas Nelson. Used by permission. All rights reserved.

Scripture quotations marked (ESV) are from the ESV® Bible (The Holy Bible, English Standard Version®), copyright © 2001 by Crossway, a publishing ministry of Good News Publishers. Used by permission. All rights reserved.

Preface

MANY CHRISTIAN COLLEGES AND universities have developed programs that allow students to serve local, national, and international communities while simultaneously learning about other cultures. Likewise, many churches and mission agencies have programs that allow people to engage in short-term assignments that provide a taste of what a longer-term assignment might be like. Whether sponsored by colleges, churches, or mission agencies, well-designed programs can offer short-term encounters that can help participants become more aware of the needs of other people in particular areas, can promote connections to local missionaries, and can encourage financial support of long-term work. Such programs have many potential benefits for the communities that are served and to the individuals who participate in these programs. Malone University, where I have been a faculty member for over two decades, supported Service Learning opportunities long before I joined the university. I have spent three summers on mission stations in Africa and have been leading Service Learning Teams since 2004. I have been fortunate to visit over thirty countries on four continents. My experiences have convinced me that participation in Service Learning Teams can be rewarding, useful, and life changing. Without adequate preparation, however, these experiences can fall short of their goals; in fact, they can actually be damaging to those we want to serve and to our own character if they reinforce consumerism, entitlement, superiority, and negative biases. One way to minimize these risks and to help us achieve the ideals of service learning is to prepare teams well and to encourage thoughtful reflection, which is the purpose of this book.

Preface

HOW TO USE THIS BOOK

This book can be used by individuals who are thinking about applying for a service learning or short-term mission opportunity, but ideally it should be read and discussed by entire teams. Team preparation takes time and effort, and this book can be used as part of that process. Several chapters would work especially well in conjunction with informational meetings when students or other prospective team members are made aware of upcoming service learning or short-term mission opportunities. Subsequent chapters could be discussed in large-group meetings with multiple teams, or could be used in individual team meetings in which the material from any given chapter could be supplemented with information relevant to a particular team. The book is structured so that it follows a sequence from application to early preparation to more in-depth preparation to reflection during and after the actual team experience. Questions are included for you to consider throughout each chapter, and these questions can be good starting points for group discussion and group exercises led by team leaders.

One of my assumptions, however, is that this book is not just about preparing for a single opportunity to learn and serve. The struggles and joys that we encounter in service learning and short-term mission teams reflect deeper issues about our own character and our understanding of what God is doing in the world. Such opportunities can provide occasions for personal insight, interpersonal growth, spiritual development, and enlarged vision. In fact, much of this book is the result of reflection on my own mistakes in leading Service Learning Teams. Many of the vignettes in this book are composites of real experiences, with details changed for stylistic purposes, to make broader points, or to protect the identity of participants.

My prayer is that this book might help readers to decide if embarking on a service learning project is a good fit for them, to assist in preparing those who choose to go, and to provide opportunities for reflection that can help make such teams effective and life changing.

In Christi glorium,
David N. Entwistle

Acknowledgments

I OWE AN UNREPAYABLE debt of gratitude to my parents, who instilled in me the importance of education, missions, and serving God faithfully with whatever talents we are given. In the words of the ancient Jewish honorific, *may their memories be for a blessing.*

I would like to express my gratitude to Celia King, Dr. Jack Harris, and Ryan Donald, all of whom have led the Center for Cross-Cultural Engagement at Malone University and have provided wisdom, guidance, and training about how to prepare students and leaders for cross-cultural Service Learning Teams. They have also been invaluable sounding boards to me and to many other team leaders when crises have arisen or curveballs have appeared. Thanks are also due to several people for reading drafts of this book: Dr. Jack Harris, Ryan Donald, and Iris McCarty.

I would also like to thank Dr. Steve Moroney and Dr. Christina Schnyders, who led a summer Faith and Learning Workshop for veteran Malone University faculty members where this project took shape. I am grateful to Malone University and to the Council of Independent Colleges, which partially supported this project through a Network for Vocation in Undergraduate Education (NetVUE) grant.

It has again been my good fortune to work with the Cascade Books in bringing this project to fruition. Thanks are due particularly to copy editor Jeremy Funk and typesetter Ian Creeger. The project editor, Dr. K. C. Hanson, has once again improved the manuscript with his editorial skills and encouragement. I would

Acknowledgments

also like to thank Mallory Adams, my student assistant, who spent countless hours collecting information for marketing.

Most of all, I would like to thank the dozens of students and colleagues who have allowed me to partner with them, and our hosts from Canton, Ohio, to Hong Kong, China, as we have endeavored to blend serving others and learning about other people and other cultures. I owe special thanks to Debbie Entwistle, Dr. Jack Harris, Dr. Mark Jakowski, Iris McCarty, Dr. Greg Miller, and Dr. Jacci Stuckey for coleading teams with me. I would also like to express my deep gratitude to Dave and Cindy Aufrance, Howard and Ave Robinson, Don and Betty Orr, Daniel and Gosia Masarczyk (and their wonderful children, Tymek, Julia, Martyna, and Jeremi), and Dr. Henryk Gasiul and his colleagues and students at Uniwersytet Kardynała Stefana Wyszyńskiego w/ Warszawie—all of whom have been incredibly gracious in working with me and with my students.

David N. Entwistle
Canton, Ohio

1

What's It All About?
Service Learning Overview

"Teacher, which is the greatest commandment in the Law?"

Jesus replied: "'Love the Lord your God with all your heart and with all your soul and with all your mind.' This is the first and greatest commandment. And the second is like it: 'Love your neighbor as yourself.' All the Law and the Prophets hang on these two commandments."

—Matt 22:36–40, NIV

WHEN I WAS ELEVEN years old, my family and I traveled to a country in equatorial Africa, where my parents spent the summer working in a hospital on a mission station. Why would anyone close a successful medical practice for three months, self-fund an expensive trip to a place that had electricity for only a few hours a day, and give up at least a quarter of their annual income? There are many layers to the answer to this question, but I think the core reason is this: my parents believed that this was the best way they could love God and love their neighbor at that point in time. And,

I think, those are really the *ideal* motives behind anything we do in life—including participating in Service Learning opportunities and short-term mission trips. But, alas, all our motives are mixed motives (more about that in chapter 2!).

That first trip to Africa opened the eyes of that eleven-year-old boy to a much bigger picture of what God is doing in the world, and to the many ways that we can love our neighbor (or fail to love our neighbor despite our best intentions—more about that in chapter 5!). It also stimulated a love of travel, cultures, and people in other lands; I have been privileged to have set foot in about three dozen countries, from Albania to Zimbabwe (the exact count is debatable since several of the countries no longer exist in the same form they did when I visited years ago).

I can't promise that joining a Service Learning Team (SLT) or going on a short-term mission trip will turn you into a world traveler, but I do think there is a pretty good chance that an opportunity of this kind has the potential to open your eyes to what God is doing in the world, in Canton, Ohio, or Canton, China; in New Orleans or New Guinea. But if you're going to go, you'll get the most out of it if you engage in thoughtful preparation beforehand. While you are on a Service Learning Team or short-term mission team, you will serve better if you develop cultural competence and plan to serve in culturally and financially appropriate ways. And you are more likely to return having experienced personal and spiritual growth and transformation if you reflect deliberately on your experiences. That's what this little book is all about—Getting Ready, Serving Well, and Coming Back Transformed. I hope that this book will stimulate your imagination and might help you see that joining a Service Leaning Team or engaging in a short-term mission opportunity might be one way of learning to love God and to love your neighbor in a deeper and more nuanced way.

WHAT IS A SERVICE LEARNING TEAM?

The first thing you need to know is what a Service Learning Team is, and, just as importantly, what it is not. At one time the Christian university where I work provided short-term mission trips. Over time, though, it dawned on us that the name was misleading. The term *mission trip* implies a very focused objective of participating in some kind of ministry as its primary or sole task. While we affirm the importance of short-term missions, as an educational institution we recognized that we also wanted our programs to be transformative experiences where students thought deeply about cultures, how to help in appropriate ways, and where they could grow in their relationship with God and their understanding of what God is doing in the world. Changing the name of our program from short-term mission trips to Service Learning Teams helped us frame this broader focus.

One purpose of a Service Learning Team is to *serve* others, perhaps working with mission agencies or local ministries, but perhaps through something that is not overtly Christian (holding babies in an orphanage, visiting refugees, loading trucks with school supplies, sharing a meal with a family). We certainly affirm that spreading the gospel and ministering to the tangible needs of others are important goals of the Christian life, but we also recognize that our impact is often maximized when we work through local Christian groups. And—truth be told—the impact we make is often quite minimal. In fact, you could make a pretty good case that if they are done poorly, short-term mission trips and Service Learning Teams have the potential to cause as much harm as good. In one sense, they are clearly financially inefficient; the money it takes to send a team could simply be given to indigenous people to meet local needs. Nevertheless, the increased cost might be justified if transformation of participants is a deliberate aim of Service Learning or short-term mission experiences.

Team preparation and reflection should be designed to foster personal and spiritual transformation of team members. If such opportunities are well constructed, Service Learning and short-term mission opportunities can expand participants' vision of what God is doing in the world. Moreover, participants should return with a better understanding of how to support and work with local ministries in ways that are appropriate and culturally sensitive. So, part of what I want to do in this book is to help you think carefully about how a Service Learning Team or short-term mission trip could be structured to be a wise and beneficial experience. We need to go with a realistic view of how we can serve in fiscally responsible ways, of how we can serve in culturally appropriate ways, and of how we ourselves can learn from others and be transformed by our experiences.

When Malone University changed the name of our program to Service Learning Teams (SLTs for short), we kept the focus on *service* but we also emphasized *learning*. This speaks to a virtue that we need to develop—*the humility and the desire to learn about and from others*. In chapter 6 we will spend time thinking about developing cross-cultural awareness, but for now we just want to point out that a major purpose of a Service Learning opportunity or a short-term mission trip that is done well is to learn about history, culture, and other people. If we are going to love others well, we need to listen to them and learn about them.

The third word represented in the SLT abbreviation is *team* rather than *trip*. You aren't just going on a trip, and you aren't going alone—you are going with a group of people who are working together to serve and to learn. Teams are good, because we really do need each other. But that can also be hard. Being part of a team means that you need to listen to the wisdom and direction of leaders. It means that you have to figure out how to work together with people who might see the world very differently than you do. And sometimes it means that you have to figure out how to work through the discomfort that happens when you and your teammates are tired, cranky, and feeling a bit out of sorts. It happens. But, that too can be a place where you can learn to love your neighbor! We'll talk more about this topic, too.

I have participated in both Service Learning Teams and short-term mission trips. Service Learning Teams are usually associated with educational institutions, while short-term mission trips are usually done in affiliation with a church or parachurch mission agency. Despite their differences, many of the same principles to effective outreach and personal transformation apply to both types of experiences, and the ideas that you find in this book have the potential to strengthen both types of programs.

This brief overview probably raises a lot of questions. Many of these questions will be covered in the rest of the chapters of this book, and you can always direct specific questions to the Cross-cultural Engagement office at your school (or whoever oversees cross-cultural learning, study-abroad program, or short-term mission teams in your local school, church, or mission group). For now, though, I hope this introduction has stimulated your appetite enough for you to begin imagining what it might be like to explore cross-cultural service, leaning, and mission opportunities.

1. What might be some differences between a short-term mission trip and a Service Learning Team?

2. How might taking part in a short-term mission opportunity or being a member of a Service Learning Team help you to love God more fully?

3. How might taking part in a short-term mission opportunity or being a member of a Service Learning Team help you to love your neighbor more fully?

4. In what ways has God gifted you that you could serve and learn in a cross-cultural setting?

5. What kind of attitudes and virtues do you need to serve others well?

6. What kind of attitudes and virtues do you need to learn about other cultures and people, and about God's work in the world?

7. What do you see as some of the opportunities and challenges of taking part in a short-term mission opportunity or of being a member of a Service Learning Team?

2

Should I Go?
Billboards, Nudges, and Wisdom

> The Lord had said to Abram, "Go from your country, your people and your father's household to the land I will show you. I will make you into a great nation, and I will bless you; I will make your name great, and you will be a blessing. I will bless those who bless you, and whoever curses you I will curse; and all peoples on earth will be blessed through you." So Abram went, as the Lord had told him.
> —Gen 12:1–4, NIV

> Then I heard the voice of the Lord saying, "Whom shall I send? And who will go for us?" And I said, "Here am I. Send me!"
> —Isa 6:8, NIV

IN THE PREVIOUS CHAPTER, I suggested that the *ideal* motives for anything we do in life is discerning that it is the best way that we can love God and love our neighbor at that point in time. Alas, I also said that all of our motives are mixed motives. Let me use my own experience as an example. My experience in Africa as an eleven-year-old child and my subsequent excursions instilled in me a love of traveling. In all honesty, one of the things that appeals to me about missionary work and Service Learning Teams is the ability to travel. I love experiencing new places, visiting museums, having friends all over the world, and—especially—eating the foods of other lands. None of these things is wrong, but just as importantly, none of them fully express the core motivation of serving God and others. Some of them could even become problematic if they become more important to me than the ideal motives. Of course, sometimes I might have motives that are dangerous—I might feel prideful that I've traveled the world so extensively, I could feel a sense of power and control about being able to tell the Service Learning Team I'm leading what to do, or I might become conceited because I am invited to give a lecture at a foreign university. So, as we think about our intentions it is important to recognize that we probably have a mixture of motives, some of which are better and healthier than others. Motives are important, so we need to embark on deliberate reflection so that we can develop insight into our motives and begin to orient them in ways that please God.

SHOULD I STAY OR SHOULD I GO? HOW HABITS SHAPE DECISIONS

Another thing that is important is the process of deciding on a course of action (in this case whether or not to apply to join a short-term mission or a Service Learning Team). Rather than looking at this particular decision, though, let's take a step back and think about decision-making in general.

Imagine that you have an important decision to make. How do you go about making this choice? Perhaps you make a list of pros and cons. Or perhaps you go with your gut—you "just know" what you should do. Then again, maybe you have no idea what to do, so you flip a coin. You might pray for guidance. Hmmm. There's an idea. But what might God's guidance look like? Does it come in the form of a billboard, a whisper, a feeling of peace, or something else?

Now, imagine another scenario. You slept well last night, and you're ready to face the day ahead. There really isn't a decision about whether or not to take a shower—that has been formed by habit. You brush your teeth, too—another healthy habit. Time to get dressed. You have some decisions to make. What should you wear? Ponder that for a moment . . .

Let's play with this scene a bit further. A lot of things that you do—good or bad—are formed by habit. As much as you might claim to brush your teeth because of the health benefits of doing so, the fact is that you probably brush your teeth because your parents trained you to do so! You might also smoke—another habit, but this time, one that is bad for you. We need to think about the way that behaviors become attitudes and habits, and actively work to create good attitudes and habits. The ways that we make decisions are shaped to a large degree by attitudes we have and by habits we have formed.

So, let's go back to our example. You've slept well, and you are about to get dressed. What to wear? Context probably matters a great deal. Are you going hiking or swimming? Is it summer or winter (and what part of the world do you live in)? Oh, is it your wedding day? Well, that changes things a bit. What are you going to wear?

The scene shifts. Yes, it is your wedding day . . . in 86 BCE. You are about to meet your spouse for the first time. Your marriage was arranged by your parents, and your clothes are prescribed by custom. One of the most important events in your life is upon you, and you didn't even have much to say about it!

The scene shifts again. It is your wedding day in the familiar time and place of your hometown. Now, how did you get to this day? You probably made a million decisions that led to this place. At some point in time, you and your about-to-be spouse struck up a conversation. Became friends. Went on a date. Perhaps broke up. Got back together. And decided that this was the person for you. And now you're ready to say, "I do." And you will go on making a million decisions that will largely determine the ongoing success of this relationship.

Because we live in such an individualistic culture, the weight of even monumental decisions is more squarely on our shoulders than has been true for most people throughout human history. As a result, we may worry more about the BIG decisions than our predecessors did. Where should I go to college? What should I major in? Should I join a Service Learning Team? Should I get married or remain single? I would argue that you were never intended to carry the burden of these decisions alone. The way we frame decisions might even lead us down some less helpful roads, so let's consider how we might think about posing good questions and making wise decisions.

So, you're about to get married. Our default mode may be to think about marriage in terms of our own potential satisfaction: will marrying this person make me happy? But what if we asked a different set of questions about marriage possibilities? Could I serve God better if I was single or married? Has God gifted me in ways that I can be a good (though imperfect) spouse for this person that I love? Am I willing and able to make a lifetime commitment to love this person? Notice that the second set of questions makes the decision less self-centered and ties the decision into what God is doing in the world and in my life.[1]

So, how we pose questions matters. But so does how we set out to answer them. So, let's think about the idea of... the CALL of GOD. Sounds pretty weighty. It is. But that doesn't mean it has to be a big mystery.

---

1. Notice too that traditional marital vows focus on loving and serving the other person in all kinds of circumstances—"to have and to hold, from this day forward, for better, for worse, for richer, for poorer, in sickness and in health, to love and to cherish, till death do us part"—rather than on personal satisfaction. Indeed, when two people really commit to such love, personal and marital satisfaction is far more likely in the long run!

Should I Go?

DECISION-MAKING AND THE CALL OF GOD

The Bible is full of stories of men and women who had very particular calls from God to do very specific things. One of the clearest calls comes early in the biblical narrative, when a man named Abram (later Abraham) is called by God to journey away from his home, to leave his father's household, and to go to an unknown land (Gen 12:1–4). Christians understandably love this story, for it is a prototype of the kind of spiritual pilgrimage that resonates with the Christian journey. Abraham's faithfulness (at least in this part of the story!) is remarkable: "So Abram went, as the LORD had told him." Wow!

And yet, when we look closely, this giant billboard of a calling is remarkably vague: Abraham was called to go where and to do what? The CALL is kind of sketchy on the details. The best we really get is, "I will show you." The pilgrimage Abraham was about to embark on was pretty scarce on specifics, but he at least knew that *God had called him*, and that *God promised to instruct him and bless him*. And let's not forget this very important detail: part of God's calling to Abraham was that "all peoples on earth will be blessed through you." Now that is a pretty amazing promise!

Abraham may have been among the first people in the Bible to have an incredible billboard-type calling experience, but he wasn't the last. Prophets often experienced very specific calls from God. Kings were anointed and given a specific set of instructions.[2] Balaam was confronted with a voice from his donkey (Num 22). The New Testament gets off to a quick start with angelic encounters to Zechariah, Mary, Joseph, and common shepherds (Luke 1:5–25; Luke 1:26–38; Matt 1:18–25; Luke 2:8–18). Jesus called twelve disciples by name to follow him (Mark 3:13–19). Saul got knocked to the ground and heard a voice from heaven (Acts 9). These are billboard-type experiences, and it would be pretty hard to miss the signs!

---

2. See Deut 17:18—one wonders how faithfully these instructions were followed.

As amazing as these experiences are, I don't think they are prototypical of the common call to follow God. Sarah went with Abraham, and apparently never received a call of her own. Many of the kings of Israel and Judah were "called" to be king merely by being the eldest son of the previous king. (But let's not forget that all of them chose whether to be faithful to the God of the Israelites or to follow another path.) David, long before he was anointed as king, became a shepherd because his father owned sheep. As far as we know, Jesus became a carpenter because Joseph was a carpenter. Thousands (no, millions, perhaps billions) of people have entered careers and marriages, that God blessed, without ever having a billboard-type experience!

Let's look at a different biblical image of faithfully responding to God. Isaiah heard the voice of the LORD saying, "Whom shall I send?" And who will go for us?" Isaiah didn't ask for a billboard, or for a miraculous sign. He just responded, "Here am I. Send me!" His response begins, not incidentally, with a declaration of his presence before God (Isa 6). Even more interesting, the very first question in the book of Genesis was directed to human beings who were hiding from God: "Where are you?" (Gen 3:9). Whereas Adam and Eve hid and shifted the blame, Isaiah announces his presence before God. Perhaps when facing any decision, big or small, it's good to remember that we are in the very presence of God. But, we need to be cognizant of this truth and open to its ramifications. (Do we need to confess sin, enter his gates with thanksgiving, humbly acknowledge his sovereignty, grieve before him as we see a broken world?) Whatever we are facing, we need to begin by acknowledging that we are in God's presence!

Isaiah doesn't seem to hesitate in response to God's question, even though the question does not seem to be directed to him. Isaiah sees a need and he puts himself at God's disposal. Likewise, whether or not we ever experience a billboard-type calling, we need to put ourselves in a position to serve God as we see the needs around us, and as we take stock of the abilities, opportunities, and resources with which God has blessed us.

Now, I certainly would not suggest that we see ourselves as obligated to meet every need that we see; no one could live up to that standard. In fact, in the midst of a busy ministry of preaching to crowds, teaching disciples, healing illnesses, feeding multitudes, and casting out demons, Jesus often withdrew into solitude and prayer. By going to one city, Jesus did not go to scores of other cities. Evidently, even Jesus didn't try to do everything or to meet every need that he saw!

We don't know much about how Jesus made decisions, but we do see him taking regular time to commune with his Father. He clearly knew the Scriptures well. (Born as a baby without language, Jesus not only needed to learn language, but he apparently had to learn the very Scriptures that in his omniscience he had ordained!). Jesus spent extended times in prayer deliberating about specific things, such as choosing the twelve disciples (Luke 6:12–16). After times of prayer and after the transfiguration, Jesus announced to the disciples that he would be killed, and he obediently and resolutely set out on the path to Jerusalem, the place where he would be tried and executed (Luke 9:51). So prayer is not at all incidental! But it might not result in a billboard either.

PRAYER AND SPIRITUAL DISCIPLINES AS A FIRST STEP

If God has not given you a billboard, you may find that he has given you some practical signposts. The first of these is prayer. In prayer, we begin to allow God to shape our attitudes. The life of prayer should be habitual—something we engage in regularly. It is one way we place ourselves before God, admitting our failures, seeking his will, interceding for others, and so forth. It will likely be one practical step by which you allow yourself to be formed so that you can discern what God may be calling you to do.

Spiritual disciplines such as Bible reading and prayer begin to shape us, but they don't usually result in specific calls to respond to particular opportunities.[3] So, we must ask, how are you supposed to make decisions? Is God's will a target with a bull's-eye in the middle? Perhaps God's will is not a bull's-eye in the way that we often might think, but it is a bull's-eye in a more fundamental sense. Throughout his Word to us, God reveals a lot of what we should do and who we should be. The psalmist asserts that we should "walk according to the law of the Lord," that we are blessed if we keep God's statutes, and that we are to rejoice in, meditate on, and delight in God's instruction, which is more precious than gold and sweeter than honey (Ps 119:103, 127). Wisdom too is said to be "like honey" (Prov 24:13–14). Is there a bull's-eye to God's will? Yes—follow his instructions! (Okay, we won't do so perfectly, and we'll need to repent often, but that's the ideal—the center of the target.) Jesus nicely summarizes the law as hanging on two commandments: "Love the Lord your God with all your heart and all your soul and with all your mind," and "love your neighbor as yourself" (Matt 32:37–39). So, a good question to ask when faced with any decision might be, would this help me to love God and my neighbor more fully? (This question even applies to issues of academia—if you are called to love God with all of your mind, what might that mean about how seriously you take your studies?) Beyond these general guidelines, as important as they are, we need some practical guidelines.

PRACTICAL SIGNPOSTS FOR MAKING GODLY DECISIONS

So far, we don't have any billboards, but we do have some good practical steps; Bible reading and prayer can help us to form attitudes and habits that allow us to be the kind of people God desires us to be. Beyond this, I would offer a number of practical suggestions that I have found helpful, taken from a book by Garry

---

3. Acts 10 records two powerful "billboard-experiences" that occurred through prayer, but remember, these types of events were rare events even for Cornelius and Peter.

Friesen. Friesen discusses seven "road signs" which may help us to make wise, godly decisions.[4]

The Bible

"The Bible," writes Friesen, "is filled with guidance that touches upon countless decisions."[5] We rightly think of some of this guidance in moral terms—the "Thou shalts" and the "Thou shalt nots." Certainly, any decision that involves or causes us to transgress the clear moral teachings of Scripture courts disaster. Beyond this, however, the Bible often talks about wisdom. It also provides examples of men and women who make good and bad decisions. We can learn from their decision-making processes and the outcomes of their choices.

Circumstances

"Open and closed doors" may help us discern our calling. Imagine that you were to apply to join a Service Leaning Team. You see an opportunity that interests you. However, the leaders who place applicants on teams offer you a spot on the New Orleans team when your first choice had been New Guinea. One door closed, another opened. At this point, you no longer need to decide about going to New Guinea—that door has closed. The fact that New Orleans is a live option does not necessarily mean that you should join that team, but it might be one means through which God is working. You also need to be wise about judging your own circumstances. As you look at your commitments, resources, and skills, your circumstances should help you determine whether or not a choice would be wise.

---

4. Friesen, *Decision Making*, 45–57.
5. Friesen, *Decision Making*, 49.

Inner Witness

"The third road sign," according to Friesen, "*is the inner witness of the Holy Spirit.*"[6] Exactly how the Spirit of God works is an open question, and different branches of Christianity subscribe to quite diverse ways of understanding this. Yet, at some level, most Christians believe that God can draw our attention to particular people, places, or needs that stay with us. We also talk about having "peace" about decisions. But a few words of caution are in order here: not every movement of the heart requires a commitment to a certain course of action (like joining a Service Learning Trip to New Guinea). Perhaps we are being led to pray for New Guinea or to support missionaries there. Likewise, while we might desire God's peace about decisions, that doesn't mean that we will be rid of all concerns or questions along the way.

Mature Counsel

Sometimes God speaks through others. People who know us well might help us to see things that we do not yet see in ourselves. For instance, professors sometimes encounter students who have never envisioned themselves going to graduate school, but, being acquainted with their work and the rigors of graduate school, a professor may encourage them to reevaluate their future plans. And the opposite is also true: sometimes students profit from wise counsel to change majors or to aim at something other than graduate school. When considering applying to join a Service Learning Team or a short-term mission, the prudent person asks people who are honest, knowledgeable, and wise for advice and feedback, knowing that God may work through others in the process.

---

6. Friesen, *Decision Making*, 52 (italics original).

Personal Desires

Personal desires are a fifth road sign. God has made you uniquely to serve him. God has gifted you with abilities and desires that can be used for his work in this world. Artists further God's work by bringing beauty into the world, and shedding light on things to which the artist's heart is drawn. Scientists help us explore the wonders of creation and to restore and shape the world in ways that honor God. Frederick Buechner, in an oft-repeated quotation, put it this way: "the kind of work God usually calls you to is the kind of work (a) that you need most to do and (b) that the world most needs to have done . . . The place God calls you to is the place where your deep gladness and the world's deep hunger meet."[7]

Although desires can be bent toward evil, if correctly understood, our desires can serve as guideposts to how God has shaped us and how he might use us in the world.

Common Sense

While certainly not infallible, common sense is a signpost that we should not ignore. There are times when we are called to do things that defy common sense—Noah building an ark in a desert, or a shepherd boy deciding to take on a giant soldier with nothing but a sling and a handful of rocks seem like bad ideas. But most of the time, common sense is a good check on our impulses. In discussing the cost of discipleship, for example, Jesus uses an analogy of someone who wants to build a tower: the wise person estimates the cost of building the tower and the resources that are available so as not to be in the foolish position of wasting resources on an incomplete project (Luke 14:28–30).

---

7. Buechner, *Alphabet of Grace*, 70.

Special Guidance

On very rare occasions, Friesen says, God may give direct guidance. As we saw at the beginning of this section, some people—like Abraham and Sarah and Mary and Joseph—receive very specific direction from God at certain points in their lives. But even in Scripture, these billboard-type experiences are not the norm. Even for the people who experienced them, they were exceptions to the rule, not the common, everyday experience. So, by all means, if you have a billboard experience that is not the product of your own imagination, then follow it. But you should not expect such signs to be commonplace or to absolve you of carefully considering how to make wise, godly decisions.

Let's return to Isaiah's encounter with God for a moment: "Then I heard the voice of the LORD saying, 'Whom shall I send? And who will go for us?' And I said, 'Here am I. Send me!'" Did Isaiah go through any of the steps that we have considered? Certainly we know that he was well versed in Scripture. This was clearly an open door. Isaiah walked through the open door to a calling for which he had been prepared. To what degree any of the other signs played a role, we do not know, but we can see God working through both ordinary and extraordinary means in the call of Isaiah.

So, how does this help you in your own decision-making process? Can these signposts help you decide whether or not to apply to join a Service Learning Team or a mission trip, or what to major in, or even what to wear? Yes! But it will not provide a billboard or a sense that you put the arrow in the middle of the bulls-eye, and that's okay! In making decisions, first and foremost, follow what you know about God's desires, and the best way to do that is to be familiar with God's Word. Second, don't extend so much time looking for billboards that you miss signposts which identify possibilities that you should carefully consider. Reflect deeply on opportunities by asking how God has gifted you and how he might be leading you to participate in his work in the world.

1. What are some of your motives for considering joining a Service Learning Team? Or, conversely, what are some of your reasons for not considering joining a Service Learning Team?

2. Think about a time when you had to make an important decision. Describe the situation and the process that you went through in choosing a direction.

3. Some people tend to obsess over decisions to the point that they become nearly incapacitated by indecision. Others tend to make decisions without carefully considering the costs and the alternatives. What about you? Describe your tendencies to overthink or to be too flippant about decisions.

4. Think about a couple habits that you have developed, one which is good for you (such as brushing your teeth or engaging in a regular time of prayer) and one which is in some ways detrimental (such as constantly being on social media or procrastinating). How did these habits develop? What reinforces them and makes it likely that you will continue to engage in them?

5. What are some habits that you would like to develop that might help you become the kind of person God wants you to be?

6. What are some of the ways that God has gifted you that could be used to love and serve others? What might hold you back or be an obstacle to participating effectively in a group that will engage in cross-cultural service and learning?

7. As you think about applying to join a Service Learning Team or a short-term mission, take some time to explore each of the suggestions about decision-making that we discussed. How can each of these road signs help you think about whether or not God might use you and shape your life through this opportunity?

    - The Bible

    - Circumstances—"Open and closed doors"

    - Inner Witness of the Holy Spirit

    - Mature Counsel

    - Personal Desires

    - Common Sense

    - Special Guidance

3

Second Thoughts and Cold Feet

> Give careful thought to the paths for your feet
> and be steadfast in all your ways.
> —Prov 4:26, NIV

> But when you ask, you must believe and not doubt, because the one who doubts is like a wave of the sea, blown and tossed by the wind. That person should not expect to receive anything from the Lord. Such a person is double-minded and unstable in all they do.
> —Jas 1:6–8, NIV

JOE AND MOE BOTH dropped out of the mission team to which they had been assigned, but for very different reasons. Joe thought that a cross-cultural opportunity would be fine—he actually liked to travel. But after the application process, he found that he hadn't been assigned to his first or second choices. In fact, he disliked one choice so much that he hadn't even put it down as an option. Why not? Well, truth be told, he had grown up in an area where people from a particular country had been gang members and thugs, and their crime sprees had hurt almost everyone that he cared about. It might not have been socially acceptable to say so, but the truth was that Joe *hated* those people. And the team to which he had been accepted was going to THAT country. He threw down the acceptance letter in disgust, determined to get as far away as possible.

Moe's reasons for wanting to quit were a bit different. He had been raised with wealth and privilege, but he had always felt like a misfit. He wanted a quiet life, out of the spotlight. But the leader of his team wanted him to take on a bigger leadership role. "No way," was his response. He came up with every excuse you could think of, and threatened to quit.

Joe is actually an Old Testament character named Jonah. God called him to be a prophet to Nineveh—the capital city of the Assyrians, people who occupied his homeland. They were brutal. Sometimes they built pyramids out of the heads of their decapitated enemies just to send a message: "Don't mess with us, or this is what will happen to you."

Moe is another Old Testament character, Moses. Although he was an Israelite, he had been raised in the courts of Pharaoh. The details are sketchy, but somehow he knew that he was Israelite despite his Egyptian upbringing in the home of Pharaoh's daughter. He killed an Egyptian slave master who was beating an Israelite slave. When he realized that news of the murder might get out, he fled across the desert and settled down herding flocks. But God had other plans for Moses, plans that Moses wanted nothing to do with.

It is interesting how often people in the Bible grudgingly accept their call. Maybe they faced bigger dangers and more discomfort than we are likely to encounter. It's pretty rare that we have students like Joe and Moe on a Service Learning Team, but it is actually pretty common that some people who could be used and shaped through a Service Learning Team never apply, and others drop out when the romanticized idea moves closer to becoming a reality.

Second Thoughts and Cold Feet

So, who doesn't apply? Interestingly, Joe and Moe have a lot of contemporary company from other guys. In my experience, with the exception of Service Leaning Teams associated with a men's varsity sport, only 10 or at best 20 percent of a typical team will be composed of young men. There are a lot of reasons for this phenomenon, and we can't really address them all here, but let's at least name this as a problem: it's harder to get men to consider applying for and committing to becoming members of a Service Learning Team, and I suspect the same may be true of both short and long-term mission assignments too.

So, Joe and Moe both wanted to drop out. We can see some pretty understandable reasons for their reluctance. While the reasons may be different, drop out is something that unfortunately affects Service Learning Teams.

CAUSES AND CONSEQUENCES OF DROPPING OUT

Imagine this: Dr. Smith has spent countless hours over many months preparing to lead a Service Learning Team to Honduras, where she has some friends who run a ministry that provides healthcare, food assistance, Bible training for pastors, and a whole lot of other offshoots. The plan is for the team to work with an English-language school and a building project. To make the trip work, they need a minimum of six students, and they can take as many as twelve. Nine people expressed interest, and after the interview and acceptance process, seven signed up. They have been meeting once a month for almost three months. An hour before their next meeting, Dr. Smith receives an email from Leo, one of the students who has agreed to be on the Team.

> Hey Dr. Smith. I've been praying about it, and I just don't feel that this trip is right for me. I hate to let everybody down, but I just really feel that God is calling me to something else. Blessings to all of you. Leo.

If you were Dr. Smith, how might you feel right now, an hour before the meeting? What might go through your mind as you reflect on Leo's email, the shrinking size of the group, and how to interact with Leo and the group around this topic?

I suspect that you might feel angry—Leo had made a commitment, and now he is backing out. Leo is also using religious language in a way that makes it difficult to talk through the conflict. (Perhaps you have heard of people who decide to back out of a romantic relationship by vaguely saying, "I sense that God wants us to break up." Well, there's a conversation killer!) Then again, Dr. Smith does recognize that God can lead people in different directions, so she doesn't want to assume that Leo is using religion as a crutch to avoid talking things through, even though she suspects this may be the case. It's also pretty irritating that Leo did this by email rather than in person, and right before the meeting.

She's also wondering what this might do to the group dynamics. And, quite honestly, losing Leo will have a major effect on the finances for the team. Everyone else will have to increase their portion of the expenses. She also realizes that if anyone else drops out, they may have to cancel the Service Learning Team altogether. What would you do if you were Dr. Smith?

She decides that, whether or not Leo drops off the team, she and Leo need to have a face-to-face conversation. It is important to talk things like this through in person. And it's important for Leo's sake that he honestly explores and discusses why he is dropping out. Perhaps things can be worked through (maybe a personality conflict with a team member, or concerns about fundraising). Or maybe he has some incredible opportunity, and there really is a fork in the road here. Then again, maybe he just isn't excited about it anymore. It might be that Leo has a pattern of not honoring commitments. As unlikely as it seems, it is possible that Leo really did have some kind of billboard experience leading him to conclude that God doesn't want him to go. In any case, Dr. Smith decides that she needs to talk this through with Leo rather than trying to respond with an impersonal email.

So, how common are Leos on Service Learning Teams? Perhaps more common than you might think, which is one of the reasons that you have to be very deliberative about a commitment

Second Thoughts and Cold Feet

to join a Service Learning Team in the first place (see chapter 2). But, after teams have been formed, it's worth thinking about why people might be tempted to drop out. Here are a few possibilities:

- *Loss of passion*—When you think about going somewhere to serve others and learn about another culture, it's exciting! But passion is an emotion that ebbs and flows, and other emotions, like fear and doubt, can creep in.

- *Fear*—Maybe what was once exciting now seems frightening. Or maybe you start to worry about what it would be like to be in unfamiliar places and eating unfamiliar food. I recall one group where several team members had never spent a day in their lives without contact with their families. Lack of daily email and phone contact was a huge deal as they realized that daily contact was not possible.

- *Relationships*—Sometimes friends apply to the same Team so that they can have a shared experience. That can be okay, but it can pose problems. People who already know each other can become a clique, and in-group, out-group dynamics are never good. So, maybe a member of the group feels left out, and decides to drop out. Or maybe the team sounded exciting when you were planning on going with someone you know, but if that person wasn't admitted to the same team or pulled out, your motivation ebbs too. Or maybe you find someone on the team a bit hard to deal with, so you avoid working through the conflict by quitting.

- *Lack of support from others*—This was a problem for Jane. She was really excited about going to Denmark on a nursing Team, but her parents really didn't warm up to the idea. Even though Denmark is a relatively safe country, they were afraid of terrorism. And Jane's boyfriend really didn't want her to be gone for two whole weeks! She wanted to go, but the lack of support was exhausting. When she talked to her team leader about dropping out, she said that she thought it would be "selfish" for her to go. Only as they explored the issue did she admit that her boyfriend told her that it was selfish for her to go and leave him behind. (Hmmm. There may be a bigger issue here, but we'll set aside questions of manipulation, control, and unhealthy relationships for now!)

- *Financial concerns*—Jessie was not financially well-off and knew that she needed to do fundraising to be able to be part of the team, but she hated asking for money. She put off writing support letters. She also became dejected when she asked for support and didn't get it. She grew so discouraged that rather than thinking about how to do fundraising, she decided to drop off the team. On the opposite side, Raven just kind of thought that she didn't need to worry about finances—God would provide, and if she didn't raise enough support, it would be okay. She was shocked when her team leader told her that she couldn't go if she didn't meet the minimum fundraising goals. So, in Raven's case, she didn't want to drop out, but it became necessary to drop her from the team because she wasn't living up to clearly articulated expectations.[1]

- *Lack of commitment*—When he applied for the team, Jack assured the team leader that he was committed to attending all the training meetings. But as the semester wore on, his schedule got filled with work and study and Frisbee golf. The meetings just weren't a priority for him. When his team leader reminded him of his commitment, he was initially irritated, but after he thought about it, he realized that he wasn't really being fair to his team and that he needed to be committed to preparation and team-building activities. Jacqui showed a similar lack of commitment, which finally blossomed into quitting because, as she put it, "Something else just came up." Some people, like Jack and Jacqui, simply have trouble sticking to commitments. They fail to come to team meetings, always have their eyes open to new possibilities, and perhaps

---

1. Knowing that people have different access to resources, we raise funds as a team, knowing that some will raise more, and some will raise less. But we clearly articulate expectations and communicate with each student during the fundraising process.

fail to realize that their choices affect other people. Here we see a lack of genuine commitment.

- **Unexpected life changes**—Sometimes, unexpected things happen that change our plans. Loved ones become seriously ill or die. People lose jobs. A family member arranges a wedding at the same time that you had other plans. There are legitimate, usually unexpected, reasons to withdraw from a Service Learning Team. Normally, these partings are accompanied by regret and grief, and it's important to process them.

I'm sure there are lots of other reasons people drop out of Service Learning Teams, and, in fairness, it is possible that God may lead someone in a different direction. But whatever the case may be, it is important to be responsible and to have an honest conversation with the team leader—and perhaps with the whole team—when someone decides to alter a commitment.

CHARACTER AND COMMITMENT

Before leaving these reflections, look back at the excuses that were offered for dropping out. In a lot of cases, these are patterns of behavior that affect other areas of our lives too. As much as dropping out of a Service Learning Team or a mission trip might have a significant impact on the team, it is also important to think about how dropping out might be a reflection of patterns that might further shape your character and affect future commitments too.

Let's go back to our opening stories about Joe and Moe. If you know the stories, you know that both of them followed through with their respective calls. Jonah went to Nineveh, but he went with a bad attitude, and in the end we see God confronting Jonah for his lack of concern for people. Moses became a great leader of the Israelites, led them out of captivity in Egypt, and wandered with them through the desert of their disobedience. God even gave the Ten Commandments through this man who tried to throw a million roadblocks in the path of God's call. Joe and Moe were imperfect leaders, yet God worked through both of them.

Recall the opening verses cited in the beginning of this chapter:

> Give careful thought to the paths for your feet
>   and be steadfast in all your ways. (Prov 4:26, NIV)

> But when you ask, you must believe and not doubt, because the one who doubts is like a wave of the sea, blown and tossed by the wind. That person should not expect to receive anything from the Lord. Such a person is double-minded and unstable in all they do. (Jas 1:6–8, NIV)

It is probably fair to say that we are more likely to stay on a path if we carefully think about it in advance, and if we attend to things that might trip us up or pull us elsewhere. The second passage occurs in the context of asking for God's wisdom. When we allow doubt to derail us, we become "double-minded" and "unstable." So, really, what we're talking about is much more important than whether or not to drop out of a Service Learning Team or a mission trip. It is actually about developing character and perseverance and consistency. For some of us—probably all of us—these things do not come easily. Let's be honest, developing these traits takes work! Recall that spiritual disciplines are part of how God forms us, so we need to engage in practices that cultivate godly character and spiritual sensitivities.

God can work through us and our doubts, fears, and failures too. But this also requires some work on our part: to be honest about what is holding us back, to identify possible solutions, and to take mature ownership by discussing issues as they arise with the people whom they might affect. It's okay to have second thoughts, but it's important to sort through those thoughts in a wise and discerning manner with people who can help you do just that. And it's okay to get cold feet; maybe all you need is a good pair of socks!

Second Thoughts and Cold Feet

1. Think about a time when you made a commitment and then backed out. Looking back, how did you get yourself into this position? Did you take on more than you should have? Did you fail to accurately and adequately assess your ability and willingness to commit? What might you have done differently to make it possible for you to keep your commitment (if, in fact, it was a commitment that should have been honored)?

2. Think about the reasons that Joe and Moe (Jonah and Moses) tried to drop out of the things to which God had called them. (You can look more deeply at their stories in Jonah chapter 1 and Exodus chapters 3 and 4.) What are some of the objections that they raised? Might you have raised similar objections had you been in their shoes? Do you have any similar excuses?

3. Why do you suppose men are less likely than women to join a Service Learning Team? Can you see other areas in American culture where men may be less committed or involved than women? How does a lack of gender balance affect a Service Learning Team?

4. Imagine that you were Dr. Smith and had just received Leo's email. How might you have reacted? Would you be more likely to try to talk to Leo or avoid dealing with this in person? Why?

5. Have you ever used (or seen other people use) religious language to avoid having honest conversation about difficult topics? Describe your experience.

6. Which of the reasons for dropping out of a Service Learning Team do you think are potential risks for you (whether in reference to a Service Learning Team or to some other commitment in life)? What can you do to prepare for and manage things so that these are less of a risk in damaging your ability to keep your commitments?

7. Imagine that someone fails to honor a commitment, and that this affects you. This might impact the amount that you have to pay for shared expenses. It might disrupt the team's cohesion and ability to work together. Describe a time when something like this happened to you, how it affected you, and how you dealt with it.

Second Thoughts and Cold Feet

8. The chapter begins and ends with a Scripture verse about *keeping your feet on the path* and another about being *tossed by the wind* and *double-minded*. Describe a time when your own indecision and lack of commitment made something difficult for you. What virtues or traits do you need to develop to be better able to choose a good path and to stick to it?

4

Let's Talk about Money

> The wicked borrow and do not repay,
>   but the righteous give generously.
>
> —Ps 37:21, NIV

> But who am I, and who are my people, that we could give anything to you? Everything we have has come from you, and we give you only what you first gave us! We are here for only a moment, visitors and strangers in the land as our ancestors were before us. Our days on earth are like a passing shadow, gone so soon without a trace.
>
> —1 Chr 29:14–15, NLT

PHIL WAS AN MK—a missionary kid. His father was an ophthalmologist who treated many people with serious optical conditions in a remote part of Africa. Paul had attended a boarding school in another country and then returned to the United States for college. After his first year in college, he tried to raise money to return

Let's Talk about Money

home and work with his parents for the summer. Despite his best efforts, though, he was well short of the financial support that he needed. But with no other options, he went to the headquarters of the mission agency the day before his flight was to leave, knowing that he could not go without a cash infusion that was not only unlikely but nearly impossible. As the other team members and their families gathered, someone made a low-key announcement about Phil's situation. The father of one of the other team members pulled out his checkbook and wrote a check to cover Phil's shortfall. When Phil went to thank the man, he simply smiled. A dozen years earlier, the man had been a missionary who had stayed in Phil's home and had broken his only pair of glasses. Phil's father gave the man an exam and replaced his glasses. Without that serendipitous encounter, he would have been completely unable to function in that remote area. "Just tell your dad this was a late payment for the glasses," he said.

This is a true story; the man who supported Phil at the last second was my father. When we went on our first short-term mission trip, my father had not thought to take a spare pair of glasses with him. At the beginning of a three-month medical mission trip, he broke his glasses. Little good would have come from a surgeon who couldn't see well enough to operate!

I could recount dozens of similar stories when God met a financial need at just the right time. But I could also recount stories of people who joined Service Learning Teams or short-term mission trips and had to drop out because they had failed to take responsibility for raising the necessary funds. Whenever we are involved in fundraising, our attitudes and beliefs about money become part of the equation, and many of us have not thought carefully about money and about how God works in that part of our life, and that is the focus of this chapter.

ATTITUDES ABOUT MONEY

Let's begin by exploring how you think about money and where you learned about money. On the blank page adjacent to this section, take a few minutes to draw a picture of some of the people, places, and institutions who taught you about money. When you think about this, though, don't focus just on things like, "My mom helped me start a savings account." Opening a savings account is certainly one kind of learning, but you also learned by observing people. For instance, you might have noticed that some people who grew up in poverty rarely eat out or, if they do, they order the cheapest thing on the menu. Money remains scarce in their minds despite present realities. Perhaps you learned about money by watching people max out numerous credit cards, always consuming beyond their means. Or you may have known people who were incredibly generous towards others even though they lived on a shoestring budget. Your drawing will likely have a variety of institutions and places (such as church, home, school, banks, and stores) and people (family and others whose financial behaviors you observed, and who implicitly or explicitly taught you about money). Your drawings may very well include contradictory messages about money.

Now, after you're done drawing your picture, spend some time analyzing it by reflecting on the following questions.

**PEOPLE, PLACES, AND INSTITUTIONS
THAT TAUGHT YOU ABOUT MONEY**

- Who taught you about money (by example or by instruction)?

- What did you learn about how to use money (or the dangers of misusing it)?

- What do the images communicate about consuming, owning, and generosity?

- How is God connected to (or disconnected from) the lessons you learned about money?

- In what ways do you think you have a healthy view of money?

- In what ways do you think your view of money is unhealthy?

Let's Talk about Money

You might be thinking to yourself, "Why are we wasting so much time talking about how I think about money? I thought this chapter was going to be about fundraising!" Well, first things first. People engage in fundraising in different ways—and do so well or do so poorly—partly because of the philosophies that undergird their view of money.

Let me frame this with an example. Imagine that Kohl has been raised in a wealthy family, and pretty much everything he had was given to him without him having to work for it. Without knowing it, he had adopted an attitude that people owe him. When it came time to raise money, he asked his parents and grandparents to support his trip and handed them donor forms. Not only did they fully fund his expenses, but they gave him a large sum of cash for personal spending. One day during the trip, Kohl twisted his ankle. The team was planning to visit a museum the next day. Kohl had become close to Suzi on the trip, so the two of them decided to ask if they could be dropped off at the mall for the day because Kohl didn't think he could keep up with the group at the museum. The leader patiently explained that they needed to stay together, but that if Kohl didn't think he could keep up with the group he could stay at the church and help with some of the projects there. Kohl erupted, "Do you think I spent all this money so I could sit around here?" Hmmm. Kohl's view of money was really all about entitlement, and it affected him and others in some pretty profound ways.[1]

Jermaine's experience was completely different. He grew up with a single mom and three sisters. He got a job when he was young and tried to help out his mom, but she refused to take money from him. They went to church regularly, and Jermaine saw his mom put money in the plate every week. When the opportunity to join a Service Learning Team presented itself, Jermaine almost didn't apply because he didn't think that he could raise the money to go. His mom, though, said, "Son, if this is what God wants for you, he will provide. You just do your part." Jermaine decided that

---

1. Notice that Kohl framed everything in terms of "his trip"—he didn't really see himself as part of a team!

he couldn't ask other people to support him if he wasn't willing to "put skin in the game," as he put it. So, he scraped from his savings to pay 10 percent of what he needed to raise. He sent out letters to almost a hundred friends and family members. He had a really good response rate, with a lot of people giving five or ten dollars, and a few giving bigger donations. Despite his own need, Jermaine gave some money to support a friend who was going on a different Service Learning Team, even though he was struggling to raise his own support. Jermaine ended up just a bit short of his fundraising goal, but a few other people on his team had been able to raise more than they needed, so he was able to go. Throughout the time of the Service Learning Team, Jermaine proved to be the one on the trip who was always looking out for everyone else, and the team wouldn't have been the same without him.

As you compare the stories of Kohl and Jermaine, there are some obvious differences in their financial means and their attitudes. But let's look a bit deeper. Kohl and Jermaine didn't just have different views about money and fundraising; they had different views about life and other people. That's why it is important for us to think about how we view money. Is money a possession or a gift? Are we entitled to use money as we desire, or do we have a responsibility to *Someone Else* for how we use it? Are we entitled to get what we want, or should we be grateful for the opportunities and the things we receive?

Now, before we leave Kohl and Jermaine, we should admit that they are, to some degree, caricatures. Many people are raised in wealthy homes to be grateful and generous, and some people raised in poverty grow up to be bitter, stingy, and possessive. And I imagine all of us can see bits and pieces of both Kohl and Jermaine in ourselves. But perhaps the biggest thing we can take from these stories is that our view of financial matters often reflects some things about our character and our desires.

BIBLICAL VIEWS OF MONEY

Not surprisingly, the Bible has a LOT to say about money. Look at the first verse that we cited at the beginning of this chapter: "The wicked borrow and do not repay, but the righteous give generously" (Ps 37:21). So, right off the bat, we see that the way we treat money can be "wicked" or "righteous." Consumerism, entitlement, greed, and a host of vices are, perhaps, our default positions. The virtuous use of money—being charitable, giving generously, and receiving with humility and gratitude—requires the cultivation of traits that do not come naturally to us. This is one of the reasons why the Bible calls us to tithe—to give a tenth of our income back to God.

Tithing is often framed as giving back to God a portion of what he has given us. Developing this habit can help to make us grateful and generous. And yet King Solomon, when dedicating the temple in Jerusalem, comments on the irony of seeing ourselves as generous:

> But who am I, and who are my people, that we could give anything to you? Everything we have has come from you, and we give you only what you first gave us! We are here for only a moment, visitors and strangers in the land as our ancestors were before us. Our days on earth are like a passing shadow, gone so soon without a trace. (1 Chr 29:14–15, NLT)

When we recognize that everything is a gift from God, and that everything we try to hold on to is temporal, it becomes easier to hold things loosely, to give generously, and to receive gratefully.

Notice that nothing we have said to this point tries to paint money or things as bad. When Christians talk about money, they rightly think about the apostle Paul's warning to Timothy: "For the love of money is a root of all kinds of evil. Some people, eager for money, have wandered from the faith and pierced themselves with many griefs" (1 Tim 6:10, NIV). Love of money, greed, and possessiveness—these are *attitudes* that are evil and empty. The author of Ecclesiastes, likewise, warns us, "Whoever loves money never has enough; whoever loves wealth is never satisfied with their income. This too is meaningless" (Eccl 5:10, NIV).

So, when you think about fundraising, recognize that fundraising can be a place where vices lurk and virtues can be cultivated; your attitudes about money are important! So with that key established, let's think about fundraising and the context of character formation.

CULTIVATING ATTITUDES OF GENEROSITY AND THANKSGIVING

Raising money to support what God is doing in the world is a noble thing, but we do need to make sure that we are raising and using money ethically. The Old Testament system of tithes and offerings was designed to support temple worship and to be part of the mechanism for providing material support for the priests and the needy. In the New Testament we see offerings taken to support those in need and to support the work of spreading the gospel. Many early Christians, especially those raised in Gentile households, had not been taught to tithe as children. Paul gave some very practical advice about developing a habit of generosity:

> On the first day of every week, each one of you should set aside a sum of money in keeping with your income, saving it up, so that when I come no collections will have to be made. (1 Cor 16:2, NIV)

Before asking others to support you, it would be wise to take stock of your own generosity. If you have not developed the habit of tithing, you should think seriously about doing so. Tithing, as I said earlier, is the Christian practice of giving a portion of your income back to God.[2] Doing so is a discipline that can help you

---

2. Christians disagree about whether a *tithe*—usually defined as giving 10 percent of your income back to God—is required for Christians today in the same way that it had been for Israelites under the Old Testament system. Setting aside those theological issues, though, the consistent discipline of tithing is a practice with benefits for our own spiritual development and for the support of God's work in the world.

avoid monetary vices and can assist you in cultivating the virtuous use of money.

In addition to tithing to support the local church and parachurch organizations, you should also ask yourself what you ought to contribute toward the expenses of joining a Service Learning Team or short-term mission trip. It is certainly reasonable to set aside part of your own income to support your own participation in a Service Learning Team. In fact, *if you aren't willing to support your own participation in a Service Learning Team, why should anyone else be willing to do so?*

A second character trait that you need to cultivate is *gratitude*. You are not entitled to anyone's support; you are simply the recipient of a gift. I recall thanking a man in my church for his support, and he responded by thanking me for giving him the opportunity to be involved in what God was doing. He understood gratitude more deeply than I did! Gratitude, though, must be developed like any other virtue. One simple way to develop gratitude is to express your thanks in verbal and written form, and to recognize the sacrifice someone makes to support you. (Note to students: this includes parents who help fund your education!)

So, let's suppose that you've decided to nurture a grateful attitude and to cultivate the habit of tithing, and that you have also decided that you will personally contribute to the expenses of joining a Service Learning Team. Chances are, you will still need substantial support. So how do you go about raising this support?

PRACTICAL SUGGESTIONS FOR FUNDRAISING

The most effective way to raise funds involves direct appeals from you to your church, friends, family members, and local businesses. So this means—gulp—asking for money! There are a number of traps we can fall into here: being too afraid to ask or being too tentative in asking, or using inauthentic or overly religious language, and . . . using poor grammar and composition. (Yep. If you are a college student, your letter should be a well-constructed composition!) Let's look at each of the fundraising risks in turn.

Being too Afraid to Ask or Being too Tentative in Asking

The first thing to look at is *why you are afraid to ask for help*. Some of us don't like feeling needy or indebted to anyone, and asking for support makes us vulnerable. Others may be afraid of rejection—*what if they say no?*—and we begin to equate someone's decision not to support us with personal rejection. Some of us are guilty of procrastination in almost everything we do, so we just put it off, which creates problems of its own.

Henri Nouwen was a Roman Catholic priest whose view of fundraising has been very helpful to me. Fundraising is not just what financially enables ministry, but it is itself a ministry. Remember when we talked about the spiritual discipline of tithing? Essentially, when we do fundraising, we are giving people an opportunity to engage in a spiritual discipline: "we are inviting people into a new way of relating to their resources."[3] We do not want to beg for money. Rather, we want to present an opportunity for others to join us in what God is doing. Fundraising for godly causes, understood correctly, is good for the spiritual life of those who ask *and* those who give. This requires first, though, that we are sure that we are inviting them to join us in "a vision of fruitfulness and into a vision that is fruitful."[4]

Imagine that you invite someone into a new way of relating to their resources by joining you in what God is doing by financially supporting you . . . and they decline. That's fine! God does not call all of us to the same ministry, or to support the same ministry financially. It might be that someone is not able to join you now—accept that fact with understanding. It might be that someone does not see this as an opportunity that they desire to support because they are supporting other ministries right now; accept that fact with graciousness. And yet, people will often be truly pleased to join with you in what God is doing by offering tangible financial support.

---

3. Nouwen, *Spirituality of Fundraising*, 5.
4. Nouwen, *Spirituality of Fundraising*, 29.

Using Inauthentic or Overly Religious Language

Imagine that you receive a letter that starts something like this: "I wanted to let you know about a ministry that God is calling me to. Lately, God has put the people of Abracadabra on my heart, and I feel called to join a Service Learning Trip to Abracadabra." As you read the letter, you wonder who wrote it. Wait a minute, she never talks like that in real life! What gives? Sometimes, we start using excessively religious language because—well—we think it sells better. "If I use real Christian-y language, they'll be more likely to support me!" Or maybe by using religious language we are attempting to prove the religious merits of what we are doing. In either case, we might be guilty of trying to manipulate people rather than simply inviting them to partner with us in what God is doing in and through us.

Now, by all means, you might well be someone who uses religious language in your everyday life. If that's the case, then using such language in a fundraising letter might well be authentic. But if you don't talk like that in daily life, then pulling out religious language in a fundraising letter might not be appropriate. My own preference in these cases is to describe in more depth the opportunity that one has—in this case, joining a group of people who will be serving in particular ways and learning about other people and their culture, language, and history—and to invite potential donors to join me through supporting me if they are able and interested in doing so.

Poor Grammar and Composition

Okay, I admit it: I sometimes have to restrain myself from correcting grammar and composition on others' Facebook posts. No, this isn't a psychological disorder; it is a mark of someone who has spent his life helping people to hone their communication skills. Few things bug me more than reading a poorly constructed fundraising letter for a team that I am leading. You are representing not just yourself but your school and your team when you send out a fundraising letter, so it should be well constructed. For this reason, I always recommend that no fundraising letters should be sent out without having been proofread and approved by your team leader. This will help to ensure that the letters are well written, that they accurately convey information about the team, and that they don't fall into any of the fundraising traps that we discussed above.

We've done a lot to set the table for writing the actual fundraising letter. So what should the letter look like? Explain the opportunity that you have. Describe what a Service Learning Team or short-term mission team is and what you will be doing. Discuss what you have been doing and how this opportunity fits into your life. Invite people to join you in this endeavor by supporting you financially if they are able to do so. Provide information about the financial need and details about how they can send donations if they choose to do so. Let them know if donations are eligible as tax deductions (the church or the parachurch or educational institution is responsible to make sure it follows IRS guidelines for nonprofit contribution and may have specific requirements you need to follow). Tell your readers that you will call them within a week to talk about your request, and that whether or not they are interested in supporting you, you want to share what's going on in your life and find out what's going on in their lives.

Who should you send the letters to, and how many should you send? I usually recommend somewhere between fifty and a hundred letters, depending on how much you have to raise and the likely ability of potential donors to support you. You should definitely approach your church; many mission committees or adult Sunday school classes are more than happy to support church members in endeavors like this. You should also send letters to family and friends. An often overlooked source, though, is local businesses. You can ask your employer, of course, but you would be surprised how often a local hardware store or restaurant or even a funeral home is happy to help out!

Make sure you start early so that you can gauge whether you need to do more fundraising. You might ask people who normally give you presents for your birthday or Christmas to instead send money to support your Service Learning Team expenses as your present for the year. You can also do fundraising activities such as candy bar sales, car washes, team leaf raking, and dinners. However, in many cases you may find that the amount of effort extended may not result in much money, so think carefully about these kinds of activities.

A CODA ON GRATITUDE

Before we leave our fundraising chapter, let's return to the subject of gratitude. You should personally contact everyone who supports you to express your gratitude as soon as possible after receiving their donations. It's also a good idea to send an email or a postcard or to keep a blog to express your gratitude and to help donors and friends participate in what God is doing in and through you as the Service Learning opportunity or short-term mission trip unfolds. You should also touch base again upon your return—more about that in chapter 10.

Finally, having been on the receiving end of others' generosity, you should also think long and hard about your own generosity. You might decide that next year you will support another student as he or she joins a Service Learning Team. Perhaps you will meet missionaries or learn about local ministries during your own team experience and decide to join them by becoming a regular supporter. Or you may be able to give back to people that your team met by providing help for a special need. Being the recipient of generosity should help us to cultivate a generous spirit!

∽

1. How would you describe your basic attitude toward money? In what ways can you see yourself being negatively affected by consuming, hoarding, wasting, or other impulses where money is concerned? In what ways can you see yourself using money wisely (e.g., by tithing and generously giving to meet

legitimate needs in ways that truly help; by living within your means; by not being wasteful; and so forth)?

2. Describe your own experiences of giving and receiving. Whether in giving and receiving Christmas gifts or fundraising, do you see yourself as someone who receives with gratitude and gives generously and joyously? How might you develop these traits?

3. What are some of your fears about fundraising? Why is fundraising hard for many people?

4. Have you ever found yourself framing things in overly religious language? In what ways might this be disingenuous or problematic?

5. What do you think of Henri Nouwen's idea that there is a spirituality to fundraising, that it can be an invitation for others to relate to their money differently and to participate in someone's ministry?

6. In what ways could fundraising help you to be a more generous person?

7. Why might it be important for you to fund part of your own expenses for participating in a Service Learning Team or short-term mission project?

8. Do you engage in tithing and giving generously to support others? If not, how can you begin to cultivate these practices? How can you wisely invest the funds God has entrusted you to support what God is doing in the world?

5

Blessings and Trials of Being a Traveling Companion

> Love must be sincere. Hate what is evil; cling to what is good. Be devoted to one another in love. Honor one another above yourselves. Never be lacking in zeal, but keep your spiritual fervor, serving the Lord. Be joyful in hope, patient in affliction, faithful in prayer. Share with the Lord's people who are in need. Practice hospitality. Bless those who persecute you; bless and do not curse. Rejoice with those who rejoice; mourn with those who mourn. Live in harmony with one another. Do not be proud, but be willing to associate with people of low position. Do not be conceited. Do not repay anyone evil for evil. Be careful to do what is right in the eyes of everyone. If it is possible, as far as it depends on you, live at peace with everyone.
>
> —Rom 12:9–18, NIV

AS SHORT-TERM MISSION TRIPS go, this was actually a pretty long one—less than a year, but more than a single semester, so it wasn't really set up quite like a Service Learning Team, but there are enough similarities that it is worth our time to learn from Mark

Blessings and Trials of Being a Traveling Companion

and what went wrong on his short-term mission trip. Mark really felt called to join this team, but he probably hadn't anticipated just how difficult it was going to be. I doubt anyone really expected things to go this badly.

To begin with, Mark was the youngest guy on this team. He didn't have the experience of the older guys. They were going to some pretty rough places, both in terms of physical conditions and in terms of the degree of hostility that they were going to face, but it was a lot easier to feel brave in the abstract than it was to face those things in real life. Add to this the fact that Mark had never been away from home for a long time, and really wasn't emotionally or spiritually prepared for all that he would face. Traveling in close quarters with the other guys on his team became a challenge. One of the other guys tried to take Mark under his wing, but, truth be told, there were tensions within the group. At times they were tired, cranky, and hungry. To be honest, they didn't have much personal space, and being in a foreign place, there was really nowhere to turn for comfort or support. Finally, Mark decided to throw in the towel. He dropped out of the group and went home.

I never had a chance to ask the other guys how they felt about Mark leaving, but I'm guessing that their reaction was less than understanding. Perhaps they were even a bit relieved. I do know that one of the guys refused to work with Mark when another opportunity to collaborate emerged. I imagine Mark felt hurt and humiliated—it had been a failure, after all. But then, I also wonder if the other guys share more responsibility for this situation than it might appear at first. Sure, Mark abandoned the group, but how well had the other guys supported him? Did they acknowledge the struggles he was having, or even validate them by admitting that this was hard for them too? Was their own machismo or their own sense of calling preventing them from recognizing the difficulties of their younger, more tenderhearted companion? I also wonder if they sometimes became irritable with each other—it would certainly be understandable if they had. I've certainly seen this happen with many teams as members become sleep-deprived, jet-lagged, and stuck in close quarters in strange circumstances.

As a leader, I've often seen it in myself. I usually get less sleep than the rest of the team because of keeping track of the budget, and because of attending to duties related to the team and to our plans and our safety; and I sometimes lack the compassion that I should have for those who are traveling with me.

So, back to Mark—or John, or John Mark. It appears that this individual went by both his common Hebrew name, Mark, and his common Roman name, John, or both in combination, John Mark. Many scholars conclude that this one individual is probably the author of the Gospel of Mark, as well as an early companion of the apostle Paul and Barnabas when they set out on their first missionary journey. In Luke's account of that journey, he includes a brief interlude about John Mark's departure: "From Paphos, Paul and his companions sailed to Perga in Pamphylia, where John left them to return to Jerusalem" (Acts 13:13, NIV). I think it was quite gracious of Luke to leave out the details of John Mark's departure. Paul's reaction to Mark's departure, though, has some hints that the departure left them on bad terms. When Paul and Barnabas prepare to leave on their second missionary journey, the tension about Mark is palpable:

> Some time later Paul said to Barnabas, "Let us go back and visit the believers in all the towns where we preached the word of the Lord and see how they are doing." Barnabas wanted to take John, also called Mark, with them, but Paul did not think it wise to take him, because he had deserted them in Pamphylia and had not continued with them in the work. They had such a sharp disagreement that they parted company. Barnabas took Mark and sailed for Cyprus, but Paul chose Silas and left, commended by the believers to the grace of the Lord. He went through Syria and Cilicia, strengthening the churches. (Acts 15:36–41, NIV)

Ouch. In fact, the word for "deserted" is even stronger in the Greek than in the English, coming from the same word as the English word *apostate*, a word we use to describe someone who has abandoned the faith. What caused such a breach between Mark and

Paul? We really don't know, but it is obvious that it was more than a minor disagreement. If even apostles can have intense conflicts, then perhaps we should be aware that this can happen to us, too.

EVEN MISSIONARIES NEED CONFLICT RESOLUTION SKILLS

A good friend of mine who is a missionary told me that part of their preparation training included classes in conflict resolution. "What a waste of time," he had thought. "We all love Jesus, we're there to spread the gospel, and we're on the same team. Why would we need to study conflict resolution?" Now a veteran missionary, he admits that it was one of the most valuable parts of his missionary preparation! We don't always share the same vision for what we should be doing. We disagree about the use and distribution of financial resources. We experience personality conflicts. We are in stressful situations, separated from our normal resources, with our ability to use our typical coping mechanisms handicapped, and we are tired. Yep. That can be a recipe for conflict. But knowing that up front can be a huge benefit because we can go into stressful situations with greater awareness that conflicts are not uncommon and with some tools to work through them.

Now, here is a secret that might help. *Sometimes, you are part of the problem* (gasp). Sad but true. And it is definitely true of me, too. It is easy to look at what other people do that irritates you, but it is quite a bit harder to realize that you might irritate others. C. S. Lewis pointed this out masterfully in his little book *The Screwtape Letters*. The book is a fictional account of a Junior Tempter named Wormwood who is receiving advice from his uncle Screwtape about how to work on his "patient" so as to ensure his damnation. Unfortunately for Wormwood, his patient becomes a Christian. But all is not lost, Screwtape assures Wormwood. One of the things that Wormwood can do is to help this young Christian to see how bothersome other people can be.

> When two humans have lived together for many years it usually happens that each has tones of voice and expressions of face which are almost unendurably irritating to the other. Work on that . . . and let him think how much he dislikes it . . . And, of course, never let him suspect that he has tones and looks which similarly annoy her. As he cannot see or hear himself, this is easily managed.[1]

Ah, yes. I have mannerisms that irritate others. How much easier it is to see that *others* have mannerisms which irritate *me*. But if I attend to my own potential to irritate others, I might first of all be more aware of this possibility and guard against it. And just as importantly, I might be a bit more humble, gracious, and forgiving when others irritate me.

So, imagine that irritation begins to brew within a team. What are some things you might do? Let's begin with what you should NOT do. Don't bottle it up. Don't gossip or complain to others.

What should you do? First, remember that one of your priorities needs to be recognizing the value of the other person and affirming the importance of relationship. This means that you need to be respectful and constructive. Second, you need to acknowledge the strain, and you need to identify what it is. But at the same time, you need to recognize that others may see things differently, and you must be willing to hear their perspectives. Rather than making accusations, try to express your experience: "I felt hurt when you said . . ." Try to understand each other's point of view. Sometimes it is helpful to listen to the other person and to restate what you heard, seeking clarification until you clearly and accurately understand each other. Be open to admitting any way that you might have contributed to the problem and apologize if that is appropriate. Explore possible solutions. If things are at an impasse, it may be helpful to talk together with a wise person who can help you find resolution.

Don't allow whatever irritation you have to fester into bitterness or resentment. Remember that you might both be tired and cranky, and you may be overreacting because of that. On occasion,

---

1. Lewis, *Screwtape Letters*, 13.

Blessings and Trials of Being a Traveling Companion

it may be helpful to give each other some space, but this should not be a way of simply avoiding conflict.

Sounds easy enough. Well, things always sound easier in the abstract. These kinds of things take practice. It would be a good idea to pair up with several people from your team and practice conflict resolution skills with imaginary scenarios. How might you respond if someone said something that you found offensive? How might you handle a situation in which a roommate on your team hasn't showered in several days and smells rather ripe? What might you say if you feel left out or excluded? Remember, in each of these cases, that you need to *listen* as well as to express your views. The goal is to restore relationship, not just to clear the air.

RECONCILIATION AND GRACE

Recall our opening story about the breach between Paul and Mark. I suspect that they both grew to regret that breach, but it also seems to have been repaired, although probably much, much later. In several of Paul's epistles it is evident that Mark is with him, perhaps even caring for him while Paul is in jail. Towards the end of his life, Paul pleads for Timothy to come visit him, and he adds this loving request, "Mark can be very helpful to me, so please find him and bring him with you" (2 Tim 4:11, NIV). I would love to know how the reconciliation between Paul and Mark took place, and how their love and respect for each other had grown. We don't know, of course, but I do have a few ideas.

First, I suspect that God was working in both of them to help them see that their relationship needed to be healed. They both needed humility and a forgiving spirit. Paul's own letter to the Romans, quoted at the beginning of this chapter, offers some further hints (Rom 12:9–18). "Be sincere in your love for others." "Love each other as brothers and sisters and honor others more than you do yourself." "When others are happy, be happy with them, and when they are sad, be sad." "Don't mistreat someone who has mistreated you." "Try to earn the respect of others." "Do your best to live at peace with everyone."

Reconciliation is possible, but it takes effort. Of course, it's better to work our conflicts out in loving and gracious ways rather than to allow a breach to occur in the first place. So, as you prepare to join your team, remember to keep an eye on your relationships. May you live well, laugh often, and love much![2]

∽

1. Romans 12 puts two ideas back-to-back: being devoted to each other in love and honoring each other on the one side, and maintaining spiritual devotion and serving God on the other. Why do you suppose these two concepts are related?

2. Look back at the story of Mark abandoning Paul on their missionary journey and the subsequent strain between them. What factors might have contributed to Mark leaving? What can you learn from his experience? What can you learn from Paul's ongoing distrust and then his later reconciliation with and valuing of Mark?

3. What might be some reasons that people on Service Learning Teams and short-term missions are particularly prone to experiencing intergroup conflict?

---

2. From a poem by Bessie Anderson Stanley in 1904 in response to the question, what is success?

4. What is your typical way of handling conflict? Options include blaming yourself and feeling guilty, gossiping, holding it in and stewing, being sullen, withdrawing from others, lashing out in anger, minimizing the conflict, talking it out openly with the person with whom you are experiencing conflict, and so forth.

5. Where did your method of handling conflict come from?

6. Imagine how you might handle an interpersonal conflict in a constructive and healthy manner. What would this look like?

7. C. S. Lewis pointed out that we are very aware of how others irritate us but often quite ignorant of how we irritate others. What are some things that you need to practice so that you don't nurse irritations that you experience?

8. C. S. Lewis pointed out that we are quite aware of things that other people do that we find irritating, but that we are strangely ignorant of our own irritating habits. What habits or mannerisms do you have that you might need to tend to in an intensive situation?

6

Increasing Your Cross-Cultural Competency

> Even though I am a free man with no master, I have become a slave to all people to bring many to Christ. When I was with the Jews, I lived like a Jew to bring the Jews to Christ. When I was with those who follow the Jewish law, I too lived under that law. Even though I am not subject to the law, I did this so I could bring to Christ those who are under the law. When I am with the Gentiles who do not follow the Jewish law, I too live apart from that law so I can bring them to Christ. But I do not ignore the law of God; I obey the law of Christ. When I am with those who are weak, I share their weakness, for I want to bring the weak to Christ. Yes, I try to find common ground with everyone, doing everything I can to save some.
>
> —1 Cor 9:19–22, NLT

Imagine that you are a Christian in about A.D. 55 or so. The church has grown beyond its Jewish roots. Remember the day of Pentecost that occurred about twenty years ago? Before Jesus ascended into heaven, he told his disciples to wait in Jerusalem for the gift his

Father would send, that they would be "baptized with the Holy Spirit" (Acts 1:4–5). Some time after this, Jesus ascended to heaven. And then, on another day, it happened. On the day of Pentecost, the disciples had gathered in Jerusalem for Shavuot, a Jewish holy day known to Greeks as Pentecost because it occurred fifty days after the first day of Passover. The day commemorated the end of the fruit season and corresponded to the change from the barley harvest to the wheat harvest. Pentecost commemorated the transition from wandering in the desert to entering the promised land and the giving of the law. Truly, this was a day of celebration!

But this year, the celebration took on a new meaning. While the disciples were gathered on Pentecost, a sound like a rushing wind was heard. Something that looked like fire appeared before them, separated, and then appeared to rest on each of them. And the Holy Spirit was just getting started!

> Now there were staying in Jerusalem God-fearing Jews from every nation under heaven. When they heard this sound, a crowd came together in bewilderment, because each one heard their own language being spoken. Utterly amazed, they asked: "Aren't all these who are speaking Galileans? Then how is it that each of us hears them in our native language? Parthians, Medes and Elamites; residents of Mesopotamia, Judea and Cappadocia, Pontus and Asia, Phrygia and Pamphylia, Egypt and the parts of Libya near Cyrene; visitors from Rome (both Jews and converts to Judaism); Cretans and Arabs—we hear them declaring the wonders of God in our own tongues!" Amazed and perplexed, they asked one another, "What does this mean?" (Acts 2:5–12, NIV)

The apostle Peter then gave a rousing sermon about the crucifixion and resurrection of Jesus. Three thousand people repented and were baptized as followers of Jesus that day!

Pentecost is sometimes referred to as the birthday of the church. Notice that it is a multicultural event; people from many parts of the world, speaking many different languages were gathered into the celebration that day. But remember, it is now twenty years later. How has this multicultural gathering panned out?

The early church struggled with cross-cultural issues on many occasions. Within a short time after Pentecost, a dispute arose because the material needs of Jewish widows were being met while those of Greek widows were being overlooked (Acts 6). Disputes would later arise about whether Greek converts needed to be circumcised and what parts of the Jewish law they needed to keep (Acts 15). God had to confront Peter with a vision so that he could transcend cultural and religious barriers that would impede the preaching of the gospel (Acts 10:9–23). Paul even found it necessary to publicly confront Peter because he discriminated against Gentile believers in the face of Jewish peer pressure (Gal 2:11–14). And Paul's attempts to spread the gospel to both Jews and Gentiles were often accompanied by difficulties, some of which no doubt involved culture and language. Over its two-thousand-year history, the church has had to learn to navigate a lot of cross-cultural issues, and it has often not done well at this.

RECOGNIZING CULTURAL DIFFERENCES

We are in the same boat that carried the early church. We need to think carefully about how to engage people from other cultures. That's one of the reasons that we emphasize *learning* in Service Learning Teams. The present chapter is designed to help you recognize, and hopefully avoid, some common cross-cultural mistakes, and to begin the lifelong process of increasing cross-cultural competency.

Imagine this. You are in another country, and someone invites you for dinner. They ask what you would like to eat, and tell you that dinner will be at seven o'clock. Sounds simple enough. It isn't.

In some cultures, asking what you want for dinner is a "filler" question—one that is designed to make polite conversation but that neither expects nor allows an answer because the menu has already been planned.[1] In other cultures, the host wants to make sure that the meal will fit your preferences, and so they really do want to know what you would like to eat. And what time should you arrive? In some cultures, showing up at 6:59 for a seven o'clock get-together is equivalent to being late, while in others showing up at eight o'clock is bordering on being inappropriately early! Some cultures are very time driven, and others are more event driven. Some cultures value task performance, while others place primacy on relationships. So, obviously, one of the things you need in developing cross-cultural competency is some understanding of the cultural expectations that govern behaviors that you will likely engage in and encounter while you are in another culture.

Let me share an example of a cross-cultural transgression that seems easy enough to manage but is actually difficult. I have been a visiting professor in Poland. Although I am comfortable orchestrating my own classes, I often feel anxious when speaking in front of large groups that are out of my familiar routine. One of my nervous habits is putting my hand in my pocket. Fortunately, one of my friends who lives in Poland told me that this gesture represents indifference to the audience. Putting my hand in my pocket would be akin to saying, "I'm not taking this very seriously, and being here with you isn't all that important to me." But, it's a habit, and my hand kept drifting toward my pocket during my presentation.

Here's another cultural difference—Americans generally educate to stimulate discussion, exploration, and critical thinking. Poles generally educate to pursue content mastery and rote memorization. So, how do I enter this foreign world? Do I ask them to adapt to me, or do I adapt to them? I've done both. When giving a keynote address at an international conference to peers, I gave a formal, content-driven lecture. When speaking to university students, I sometimes begin by acknowledging the cultural differences in education and asking them to pretend to be American students for the day and to interact with me. (On one occasion, a Polish student came up to me after my lecture to tell me that

---

1. This is the case in many Gulf Arab states; see Risse, "To Learn Arabic."

he had never realized that education could be fun!) Now, as an American, it's easy for me to look at these scenarios and to see my familiar American educational paradigm as better than the Polish one. But is it? Polish students are generally much better at memorizing facts and details than my American students. A Polish teacher once told me that she wanted her students to learn confidence and self-esteem from my students because her students were too self-effacing. I cringed a bit. Sometimes, Americans are too full of self—we are self-assured, self-confident, and self-promoting. Perhaps my students and I could learn a few things about humility, gratitude, and hospitality from our Polish peers! We need to be attuned to cultural differences and to guard against our natural bias to privilege our familiar cultural norms.

CULTURAL AWARENESS AND CULTURAL SENSITIVITY

One of the most common cultural faux pas for Americans traveling abroad is how we present ourselves to others and how we act in public—we are often loud, demanding, and excessively casual by the standards of many cultures. We talk loudly, and we all talk at once, whereas people in many other cultures prefer carefully and quietly attending to one another and maintaining a respectful moderation of the volume of conversation, especially in public settings. We are often demanding. An advertising campaign for an American hamburger chain once proclaimed, "Have it your way." In many countries, asking for changes to a menu at a restaurant is considered rude. We like our sandals, shorts, and T-shirts, and spaghetti straps—all of which communicate disrespect and slovenliness in many parts of the world.

"But that's just who I am. They need to accept me for who I am." That attitude is the epitome of American individualism. But guess what? *It's not all about you. It's not all about your comfort. It's not all about your preferences, your desires, your happiness, or making others accept you.* Cultural sensitivity requires that you first develop cultural awareness (i.e., that you understand the culture

The Service Learning Book

that you are entering), and that you adapt to its standards. But, there are exceptions.

I was once leading a trip to another country that had much more strict codes of dress than we do in the United States. One of the young women on the trip asked if she should remove her eyebrow piercing. "I don't know. Let me ask," I said. When I talked with the local missionary, he said that it would, indeed, be a cultural issue, but he advised in this case for her to keep her piercing anyway because—and this is key—he knew that this was something that local Christians needed to think through. Sure enough, the local people ended up having a discussion about whether or not someone could really be a Christian and have an eyebrow piercing! Now, here's an important observation. The young woman was quite correct to ask if she should remove her eyebrow piercing out of respect for a different culture rather than insisting that her hosts needed to accept her as she was. But having checked it out with her trip leader and with local people who knew the culture, she was told it was okay to violate a cultural norm because there was a bigger issue here that would be raised by her appearance, which wise people close to the situation were prepared to navigate.

This was quite different from a situation that occurred a few years later in the same church when a young man failed to bring culturally appropriate church attire and went to church in short blue-jean cutoffs, a T-shirt, and flip-flops. This young man had disregarded explicit instructions on how to dress in the host culture, creating a situation in which he was seen by the local people not only as dressing inappropriately but as being disrespectful. In the instance of the young woman with the eyebrow piercing, some of the women in the church kissed her on both cheeks when she left, communicating their love and affection for her while having worked through a cross-cultural issue. In the second case there was no such affection for the young man who came to church in a way that was seen as disrespectful.

In the examples discussed above, notice how important attitude is. Having the humility to ask about possible cross-cultural issues is important. The willingness to listen to the instructions of trip leaders, local contacts, and others is imperative. Cross-cultural mistakes and misunderstandings are inevitable, but displaying healthy respect for others' beliefs and customs goes a long way toward bridging these gaps when they occur.

IMPROVING YOUR CROSS-CULTURAL COMPETENCE

In order to help you improve your cultural competency, your team will probably discuss readings about cross-cultural issues, educate you about the culture you will be visiting, and engage in some cross-cultural exercises. In this last section of the chapter, we will discuss a framework for developing cross-cultural competence and suggest a few exercises that might help you to think about cross-cultural issues in your own backyard.

When we prepare teams for cross-cultural experiences, we provide a rubric that helps them assess their cross-cultural awareness and competency.[2] The first level of cross-cultural awareness is being unconsciously unaware. In this stage, a person is oblivious to the presence of cross-cultural issues. Rather than preparing for anticipated and unexpected cross-cultural differences, the person in this stage merely reacts to events as they occur. The person in this stage tends to assume that their own cultural stance is correct and that the other cultural stance is inferior or even wrong. To whatever degree cross-cultural awareness does occur, it tends to look like pity at best or superiority at worst, and it is characterized by an unwillingness to change. Common reactions to cross-cultural differences from a person at this stage might be seen in statements like the following:

- "I've had Chinese food before, and it wasn't anything like this!" (This was actually overheard at a restaurant in China!)

---

2. These four stages are adaptations of Broadwell's four stages of learning new skills (competencies). Originally, this framework was not applied to cross-cultural competency.

- "They don't have ranch dressing in Ireland? Well, they should!"
- "It's so good that we can be here to help these poor people!"
- "This trip really made me so grateful to be an American."
- "This picture will look so cool on Instagram!"
- "That's dumb. That's not how we do it back home."

Notice how each of these responses lacks cultural humility.

In the second stage of cross-cultural awareness, consciously unaware, a person becomes aware that there are cultural differences and norms. Although she may have difficulty identifying cultural norms, she is motivated to learn more about them. She asks questions and tries to observe differences. She desires to interact with people from other cultures. The following statements reflect this level of cross-cultural awareness.

- "I really don't know much about other cultures, but I think that we should learn about how other people live and what they believe."
- "Everyone is made in the image of God, and it is important for us to try to understand the diversity that exists within the human family."
- "I would like to learn about and experience other cultures."

Notice that this level includes more cultural humility and cultural appreciation. The second stage is also characterized by a dawning recognition of a steep learning curve toward cultural competence.

The third stage of cross-cultural awareness, being *consciously aware*, forms when people engage other cultures and begin to reflect on cross-cultural experiences in ways that are deeper than just being cognizant of difference. In this phase, people begin to be mindful of different cultural norms and make efforts to adapt to them in appropriate ways. Engaging in cross-cultural experiences is intuitively meaningful and yet uncomfortable in that it does not come naturally, and it may upset our preconceptions. In this phase we begin to ask deeper questions about other cultures and to reflect more deeply on our own culture with more cultural humility. This stage is marked by a growing desire to know others more intimately and to participate in their hurts and hopes and fears and joys. This phase often involves uncomfortable reflection on ways that the attitudes and history of your own country may contribute to problems in other parts of the world in economic, military, political, and other ways. The following statements might be typical for someone in this stage:

- "I have been shaped by my culture in ways that I have not been aware of, and I may need to reconsider some of my beliefs and ways of acting in light of what I have learned and experienced."
- "I didn't realize that when we sent clothes to Haiti, thinking that we are helping poor people, we ended up putting tailors out of work and causing harm. There has to be a better way of making sure that our desire to help doesn't hurt people."
- "When we went to the concentration camp, I realized that a lot of the soldiers were barely more than kids. They were my age. They did awful things and then they went home to their families. How can someone be a loving father and a brutal killer? They were ordinary people shaped by an evil culture. What does it mean that good and evil reside in all of us and that evil can be constrained or unleashed by a culture?"
- "I've met some people during this experience that I have come to care about. I really want to get to know more about them. I've even been thinking that I should take some language courses and learn more about their history and culture."

Notice that in this phase we continue to see humility, but the desire to learn about others and to reflect deeply about cultural issues is much more pronounced, and that it might disturb one's assumptions and comfortable naiveté.

The fourth phase occurs when someone becomes *subconsciously aware* of cultural issues. In this phase, a person automatically adjusts her thinking and behavior in appropriate ways to adapt to cultural differences. She initiates cross-cultural contacts with others and openly acknowledges cross-cultural differences in ways that allow for both deep appreciation and critique of cultural norms. She senses things of value in other cultures that she has incorporated into her own life, even when she is in her native culture. She is able to point out and respond to cultural injustice without being defensive. She seeks to ensure that she empowers others rather than creating dependency, and that she helps others in ways that are not harmful. Characteristic ways of responding might include the following:

- "I realized that we Americans are far too dependent on our automobiles. I used to hop in my car to go from class to chapel and back. There's plenty of time to get from one to the other, and walking is a better use of resources and it allows me to talk to others and get some exercise rather than rushing all the time."

- "I used to think that people in poor countries were just lazy, but it isn't that simple and my views were really judgmental and inaccurate. There are so few economic opportunities there. It takes real courage to try to find work outside of the drug cartels. And the cartels are largely fueled by American consumption of illegal drugs. I've decided that supporting ministries that help people with education, training, microloans, and help with exports is a worthy cause. Spreading the gospel certainly involves telling people the good news about God's love, but it also involves efforts to bring about justice and to provide for the material needs of people that God loves."

These comments indicate a much deeper humility about complex issues that contribute to injustice, and careful thinking about how we can help and the risks of doing things that make us feel good but that contribute to injustice and waste. People who have developed the highest levels of cross-cultural competency easily and naturally adapt to cultural differences.

Even people who live and travel cross-culturally on a regular basis do not always function at the highest levels of cross-cultural fluency. And you certainly will not attain this just by participating in a Service Learning Team for a few weeks or even a short-term mission that lasts for months. But you can nudge yourself a little further, shaped by humility and a desire to grow in your cross-cultural awareness.

PRACTICAL CROSS-CULTURAL EXERCISES

Before you enter a foreign culture (which includes many subcultures within the U.S.!), I would like to suggest that you engage in the following exercise just to get you started. Even most small cities feature places where you can learn about other cultures. In my current hometown are a Chinese market, a Hispanic market, and an Italian market. They are quite authentic, catering to immigrants who have settled in the area. And within an hour are a Russian and Eastern European market, a Korean market, Chinese markets, and so forth. Whenever I'm preparing a team for a cross-cultural experience, I have students go to these markets in groups of two or three. They need to buy some inexpensive edible item—which we will share as a cultural treat at a meeting. But we also use the experience to think about culture. What kind of foods do they carry? What do the foods and beverages tell you about the culture? How are items displayed? What language(s) are things labeled in? Are things priced in different ways than you are used to? Do you hear people speaking different languages? This is just one way that you can seek out cross-cultural experiences as you begin to develop cross-cultural awareness. You might also try going to a worship service in another language.

CULTURE AND LANGUAGE

One last observation needs to be made: true cross-cultural competence is unlikely without linguistic fluency. That reminds me, unfortunately, of a riddle: What do you call someone who speaks three languages? Trilingual. What do you call someone who speaks two languages? Bilingual. What do you call someone who speaks one language? An American.

There is incredible benefit in the fact that so much of the world speaks English as a second language. You can travel to most of the world's large population centers and get by just on English. Many international businesses and industries utilize English as a common medium so that people from different nations who speak different languages can communicate in this common language. (Imagine how important it is that airline pilots and air traffic controllers around the world use English as a common form of communication!) But there are also drawbacks to this system. The assumption that we can expect people to talk to us in our language easily leads to a sense of entitlement. Because the United States is such a large country where English dominates the landscape, we have little incentive to learn another language, and our educational system typically does not offer foreign language classes until we are past the age to learn easily and so to become fluent.

You may not learn more than a few words of another language on a Service Learning Team, but you should at least recognize with humility how fortunate you are that other people have extended to you the grace of learning your language. One of the things that I love about traveling is the opportunity simply to hear other languages, and especially to be in worship services where I can hear others singing, praying, and talking in other languages to God, who hears and understands the entire human family. Such situations always seem to me to be a glimpse of heaven, as seen in this picture from the book of Revelation:

> After this I looked, and there before me was a great multitude that no one could count, from every nation, tribe, people and language, standing before the throne and before the Lamb. They were wearing white robes and were holding palm branches in their hands. (Rev 7:9, NIV)

Now *that* is a picture of cross-cultural celebration! People from all over the world gathered in white robes (symbolizing purity),

Increasing Your Cross-Cultural Competency

holding palm branches (symbolizing peace), worshiping God in every language. What a beautiful picture that is!

∼

1. Think about a time when you witnessed cross-cultural insensitivity (whether or not it involved you). What tipped you off that a cultural issue was in play? Did other people notice the conflict? How might it have been avoided or resolved amicably?

2. Describe some cultural differences that you have noticed in various religious settings.

3. What can we learn from the ways that the early Christian church tried to navigate cross-cultural conflicts and religious standards?

4. Imagine that you become aware of a cultural difference that might offend others. How can you check this out and determine an appropriate course of action?

5. Many Americans return from other countries with a heightened sense of their own superiority (saying, e.g., "I'm so glad I'm an American!") Why is this problematic? How can we be appropriately grateful for our country and its culture while simultaneously learning to critique parts of our culture that may be unhealthy?

6. In what ways can you see yourself as *unconsciously unaware, consciously unaware, consciously aware,* and *subconsciously aware* of cultural issues? What can you do to improve your cross-cultural competence?

7. Attend an event or visit a place where you are likely to encounter people from a different culture. Describe the experience.

8. Why do you suppose the Bible depicts heaven as a place where there are people "from every nation, tribe, people and language" rather than as a place where such cultural differences are minimized or eliminated?

7

Packing Lists—
Don't Forget Your Passport!

> Then Jesus asked them, "When I sent you without purse, bag or sandals, did you lack anything?"
> "Nothing," they answered.
> He said to them, "But now if you have a purse, take it, and also a bag; and if you don't have a sword, sell your cloak and buy one.
> —Luke 22:35–36, NIV

WHEN WE LEFT THE university, I ran through a checklist with my team. Suitcases—check. *They already had a packing list, and we had distributed items that we needed to take to team members to be packed in their suitcases, so hopefully they followed their instructions.* Carry-on baggage—check. *Hopefully they had followed the advice to put medications and any other items that might be needed during travel in their carry-ons as instructed.* Tickets—check. *I was keeping all of these together until we got to the airport.* Emergency first aid kit—check. *I hate carrying this, but past experience has convinced me that its worth having along.* Passports—check. *All present and accounted for.* We got through check in, baggage check, and security without a hitch. The first flight was perfect. We had gathered our belongings and arrived at our departure gate for our flight from Toronto; two more flights to go. We settled in for the two-hour wait. And slowly, panic erupted.

I first noticed some intense conversation. Then some frantic searching. And then the bombshell dropped, "Dr. Entwistle, I can't find my passport!" More searching. A mad dash to the previous gate and plane. Inquiries made to the airline. Finally, we decided that we would have to go on without one team member, but we were in Canada, and she couldn't return to the U.S. without her passport! And she hadn't brought her driver's license, which would have at least been a form of identification. Phone calls were placed to the student's parents and to the school to do some brainstorming. It was almost time to board the next plane. I sprinted back to the previous gate one last time. And there it was, in the hand of a helpful airline attendant. The student had placed her passport in a sleeve of her duffle bag and it had fallen out in the overhead compartment of the airplane where no one would ever have seen it. Anxiety. Relief. Irritation. More phone calls. *Don't forget your passport!*

"Don't forget your passport" doesn't just mean to make sure you have it at the airport; it means that your passport should *always* be in a secure place from which it can easily be retrieved but not easily lost or stolen. That was one lesson I learned with this one particular team.

PREPARING FOR POSSIBLE PROBLEMS

Previous teams had convinced me that we should always travel with a first aid kit. We've used chemical ice packs, ace bandages, band aids, Advil, Tylenol, aspirin, Benadryl, hand sanitizer, bug spray, itch and burn relief lotions, alcohol pads, and just about everything else in the kit on one trip or another. Well, we haven't used the whistle—yet. Basic first aid training has come in handy often enough that I consider it a must for at least one person on each team to have first aid training and a first aid kit.

We check weather forecasts and State Department advisories, and we plan accordingly. Despite careful planning, we have had teams affected by hurricanes, volcanoes, political coups, and broken bones. Unfortunately, if you send a lot of teams to a lot of places over a great many years, you will encounter some pretty interesting things, so you had better be prepared.

First, you need to look at likely threats that cannot be avoided. At Malone University, we always check to see if the Centers for Disease Control recommend particular vaccinations, and we pass those recommendations on to our teams. Second, we always check with the State Department to make sure that there are no travel alerts that should alter our plans. Third, we always take steps to stay together and to try not to stick out as tourists. Fourth, we always have some basic first aid training. Fifth, we engage in how-not-to-have-a-crisis training—we want to head off and avoid crises rather than having to respond to them! Sixth, we establish protocols for emergency communication with school officials and family members if necessary. Seventh, we know that emergencies can occur, so we always pay for international travel medical insurance, which can be purchased in inexpensive weekly increments. Eighth, we always carry a folder with copies of every team members' passport, emergency contact information, and medical history (including medications and allergies). Every member of the team has a copy of emergency contacts, our itinerary and flight numbers. These are just a few of the things we do to prepare our teams and our team leaders.

Preparation is about a lot more than packing lists and passports, but, fortunately, most teams have fairly routine travels. So, let's talk about packing.

PACKING FOR SERVICE LEARNING AND SHORT-TERM MISSION EXCURSIONS

Unfortunately, there is no "one size fits all" packing list for a Service Learning Team or a short-term mission trip. What you need to take and what you need to leave behind will depend on the team's purpose, the length of the stay in the host culture, and the unique circumstances each team will face. However, following these general guidelines and consulting the sample packing list below are good places to start.

First, it is important to note that the purpose and length of the experience has to drive even the packing list. Look at the passage of Scripture at the heading of this chapter. In it, Jesus is giving his disciples instructions about packing! He had once sent out his disciples in pairs, and he told them, "Take nothing for your trip except a walking stick. Take no bread, no bag, and no money in your pockets. Wear sandals, and take only the clothes you are wearing" (Mark 6:8–9, ICB). Talk about minimalism! Why would Jesus send out the disciples with virtually nothing but the clothes on their backs? Probably because the purpose of that trip was to teach them to rely on God. But now Jesus is sending them out again. This time the purpose is different, and the packing list is more extensive: money, a bag in which to stow a few things, a sword (and, I'll admit, that last one always puzzled me a bit!). But it's still a pretty small packing list!

One of the biggest mistakes people tend to make in preparing for Service Learning Teams and short-term missions trips of relatively short duration is *over*packing. I have been on a team where each student brought two large suitcases to a place where the average local person owns two changes of everyday clothing and one set of dress clothes for Sunday. Hmmm. What do you suppose it looks like when the American twentysomethings show up with more belongings in their suitcases than their host families possess? We have since limited team members to one checked bag and one carry on bag.

Packing Lists—Don't Forget Your Passport!

Another reason to pack light is because you have to carry all of your stuff everywhere you go—through airports, up flights of stairs, on the mile-long hike from the hostel to the train station. And you have to store the stuff—on the plane, on the train, in the taxi, on the city bus. Do you really want to do this to yourself?

In many parts of the world, clothes are reworn, and washed every few days. So, the first thing you should ask yourself is, "How much stuff do I really need to take?"

Okay, what do you REALLY need? *Don't forget your passport* (I'll bet you saw that one coming). Any medication that you need is a priority, and it should be packed in your carry-on bag in original prescription bottles. You should take a reasonable amount of spending money. What's reasonable? Remember, you aren't going on a tourist trip to load up on souvenirs, but that doesn't mean that you can't enjoy a cup of coffee, purchase a few small thank-you gifts to take back to family and friends, buy a few mementos for yourself, and so forth. Talk with your team leader about what is a reasonable amount of money for where you will be, and about any expenses that you will need to cover for yourself. (For example, some teams might plan for a day when you are on your own, so you might have some meals that need to come out of your pocket.) Again, a reasonable amount of spending money can differ wildly: in some countries you might need forty dollars per person for a cheap lunch while in other places forty dollars could buy a nice dinner for the entire team.

Thank-you gifts—depending on the culture your team will be working in, it may be culturally appropriate to bring some small thank you gifts for host families or people you will be working with. Again, this is something that you should talk to your team leader about.

Obviously, the time of year and the weather will be the major drivers for what kind of clothing you take. You also should ask about what kind of clothing is culturally appropriate. In Italy, for instance, women cannot enter a cathedral with bare shoulders or exposed knees. In much of the world, going to church in shorts, a T-shirt, and flip-flops would be a major no-no, while in many developing countries that are very hot, shorts and a T-shirt might be quite appropriate. Again, the key is to ask your team leader and to plan accordingly.

Below is a sample packing list that I use when I take teams to Poland. Your own list will differ based on local cultural norms, weather, the tasks that you will be engaged in, and so forth.

PACKING FOR POLAND

Have your passport, luggage, and carry-on items ready to go, tags on bags. We will tie identical ribbons on our bags to make them easy to identify.

General Suggestions

- One carry-on with one change of clothing, toothbrush, medicines, etc. It should include anything that you would not want to go without if your luggage is lost. You are allowed one carry-on and one personal item, such as a laptop or purse. I would recommend one medium to medium-large checked bag. A small backpack is handy for day trips. Weight limit is fifty pounds—if over, YOU have to pay a hefty baggage fee!![1]
- Check the weather forecast before packing—May in Poland can be really cold or really nice.
- Think about layers of clothing—it's easier to add or remove layers of clothes than it is to take a range of light to heavy clothes. Choose a coat that fits the weather forecast.
- Take good walking shoes. We will be doing a LOT of walking! Do not try to break in a new pair of shoes on the trip. NO FLIP-FLOPS.

1. Note: Travel regulations change regarding what can be transported in carry-on and checked baggage, as well as the weight limits, so check with your airline for current guidelines. Also, when returning to the U.S., make sure that you are prepared to fill out any necessary customs and declaration forms and make sure that you are not transporting any forbidden items.

Packing List

- Bible
- Journal and pen
- Passport
- Driver's license (no, you won't be driving, but a second form of ID can come in handy if you lose your passport)
- Student ID (this may get us discounts on some admissions)
- Medicine
- Toiletries (shampoo, conditioner, and the like). DO NOT BRING HAIR DRYERS.[2]
- Electricity adapter / converter
- Camera, phone, charger. (NOTE: You will have Wi-Fi access occasionally.)
- At least one set of grunge clothes and pair of shoes for work projects
- At least one nice outfit and pair of shoes for church, university.
- Good walking shoes
- Five or six outfits in total (including what you wear on the plane)
- Sleeping attire
- A few single-use packs of Woolite (if you want to hand-wash a few items during the trip)

---

2. On one occasion, some students failed to listen to this instruction. They plugged a normal U.S. hair dryer into an adapter, and turned it on. The hair dryer not only blew up, but it also took out the power for the entire church building where we were staying. Unfortunately, the church was having a baptismal service that day, and, as a result of the students failing to listen to instructions, the baptism took place in unheated water, and everyone who entered the water came out shivering!

- Towel and washcloth—you may need a towel depending on our accommodations; we will confirm this as we finalize our plans.

Leave room and weight for things to take (e.g., gifts and other things) that we will distribute among team members.

Cash

We will provide meals and water. If you wish to buy snacks, soft drinks, souvenirs, and so forth, these will be at your expense. In Poland, it is easier to convert cash into złoty. In airports and major stores you can use credit or debit cards. Notify your credit card company that you will be traveling out of the country (otherwise, they may block your account due to "suspicious activity"). Cash is sometimes the only way to buy things from street venders and in small shops, so we will exchange U.S. dollars for Polish złoty when we get there.

~

As was noted earlier, your own packing list may be quite different based on where you are going, what you will be doing, the weather, and cultural norms, but this list should at least give you some guidance on how to think about packing. Remember, one of the most important keys is to pack light. Imagine trying to lug two fifty-pound suitcases up four flights of stairs, and you may suddenly realize that there is a lot that you can do without! And above all else, *don't forget your passport!*

~

Packing Lists—Don't Forget Your Passport!

1. Jesus gave very dissimilar packing directions to his disciples on two different occasions when he sent them out to spread the good news. Why do you suppose the packing lists were so different?

2. In general, American students tend to overpack when going on Service Learning Team excursions. What do you think our tendency to overpack says about our culture and our values?

3. Imagine that you are a person who lives in a country where most people only have one or two changes of clothing, and a group of Americans shows up, each carrying a couple of fifty-pound suitcases. How might you react to this situation? In what ways might this hinder their work with you?

4. Look over the sample packing list in this chapter (pages 76-78). As you think about the team that you are joining, make a list of things from the sample packing list that will likely remain the same, and a list of things that will likely need to change.

5. How can you make sure that you keep track of your passport at all times?

6. What kind of situations should you make sure you are prepared to handle during your Service Learning or short-term missions trip? What can you do to prepare in advance?
    (*Note*: Simulations are always preferable to just reading or thinking about these things—we learn a lot more in simulations because we can identify some of the things that we might do wrong in an emergency, and we can develop protocols that we have followed in practice situations.)

7. Some people would argue that you should just "trust God," and that the more you prepare, the more you are showing a lack of faith. In what way does that advice rest on bad theology?

8

Whatever You Do . . .

> Whatever you do, work at it with all your heart, as working for the Lord, not for human masters, since you know that you will receive an inheritance from the Lord as a reward. It is the Lord Christ you are serving.
>
> —Col 3:23–24, NIV

> We have different gifts, according to the grace given to each of us. If your gift is prophesying, then prophesy in accordance with your faith; if it is serving, then serve; if it is teaching, then teach; if it is to encourage, then give encouragement; if it is giving, then give generously; if it is to lead, do it diligently; if it is to show mercy, do it cheerfully.
>
> —Rom 12:6–8, NIV

BECAUSE THIS BOOK WILL be used by many Christians doing many different kind of things, it cannot include specific information about what you may be doing on your Service Learning Team or short-term mission team. Some teams may engage in explicit

Christian ministries, such as evangelism, running Christian youth camps, leading Christian marriage retreats, engaging in pastoral training, preaching in churches, and so forth. Many teams, however, are engaged in helping the local church meet local needs by, for example, holding medical clinics, caring for displaced people in refugee camps, teaching English as a second language, or doing construction projects. When engaging in overtly Christian ministries, it is easy to see the connection between ministry and the activities that the team is engaged in, and team members often feel good that they are trying to meet spiritual needs. When teams are involved in services that are not explicitly linked to overt Christian outreach, some members may feel unsettled, as if what they are doing isn't *really* ministry. Let me illustrate some of these tensions with a brief story.

Jennifer had been on many short-term mission trips. Every year, her local church sent a group of people—mostly youth group members and a few adults—to an orphanage in Central America. They spent months raising money, collecting clothing and school supplies, and preparing skits to tell the gospel story. Since none of them spoke Spanish, their best ways of communicating were through nonverbal skits and interactive games. Coloring, drawing, playing soccer, and eating together were their main forms of communication. They did have an interpreter, which was very useful when one of them preached or shared a testimony in church. Jennifer came to love these trips. She was pained by the hardships that the children in the orphanage encountered. She enjoyed seeing the smiles on their faces, and she felt so good when she could tell her church family how many children got saved in the public services during each of the trips.

What Jennifer didn't know, however, is that the orphanage was visited by several church groups every year. The same thing happened every few months—a group of Americans dropped in, legitimately wanting to help those who were in need, but having given little thought about what would be helpful. Each group played with the children and presented the basic gospel message, but no one was there to engage in discipleship. The director of the orphanage, Isabel, appreciated the supplies that each church brought. In truth, though, Isabel and her small staff found that the church visits sometimes created problems: the children bounced between being the center of attention when these teams were present and feeling depressed and neglected when they settled into the normal routine. Isabel also knew that their long-term prognoses were not good. Many of the children would sooner or later leave the orphanage and eventually end up on the street: some would turn up in prison, and some would become trapped in prostitution. A few would get jobs in a resort catering to Western tourists on the coast, but the truth was that there was little hope that life would improve for most of these children. Isabel was grateful that she could create a safe space for a few years, but the factors that led to these children's abandonment and to their long-term hopelessness were overwhelming.

In college, Jennifer couldn't wait to go on another trip. She signed up for a team that was going to the Middle East. During their excursion the group spent time becoming immersed in the local culture and learning about the people, history, politics, and economics of the region. Their service projects involved cleaning up a local park near the church, painting some rooms in the church building, and participating in the church's outreach to the community through an English café. People in the community wanted to go to the café where they could practice English because the ability to speak English well was a marketable skill. The local church had found that running an English café was a great way to build relationships. Over time, several people had begun talking about difficulties in life with some of the church members. As a result, some of them began to attend the church.

Jennifer did not enjoy her time with this team. She didn't think of what she was doing as ministering to people. There were no evangelistic services. There were no tangible needs to be met or children to play with and hug. She wasn't able to return home and report how many people got saved. When she was with her church group, she felt like she was making a difference; here, she felt more like a tourist.

WHAT CONSTITUTES EFFECTIVE MINISTRY?

Jennifer's reactions in Central America and the Middle East are complicated. She clearly wanted to help people, and she invested a great deal of time and effort into trying to do so. Unfortunately, her first group was led by a desire to help but without thoughtful deliberation and conversation with local leaders about what would be helpful. The impulse to help is good! But the impulse to help must be tempered by knowledge of what will be helpful. Workers in disaster response are very familiar with this phenomenon. Following a mass disaster, people want to help, and sometimes they demonstrate this by sending teddy bears for children. But these unsolicited gifts often become a problem. In one school shooting case, a town had to rent warehouses to store all the gifts that had been sent to the town, very few of which were actually needed or useful.[1] Additionally, we sometimes help in ways that are very inefficient, such as collecting bottled water and paying to have it sent to a far-off disaster site, when one could have sent money to purchase bottled water nearby for a fraction of the cost. People who send teddy bears and water in such circumstances often feel good, but what they did may not be optimally helpful, and might even be harmful.

One of the things that Jennifer struggled with is that she did not have a clear idea of what ministry and service should look like. Her work in Central America made her feel good. But we cannot judge success merely by the feelings evoked within us. In fairness, this was not Jennifer's fault—she was young and impressionable. It would have been good, though, if the adults who led the trip had done some detailed research on what the local needs were, what local resources were available, and what resources could not be obtained locally. The church leaders would have benefited by

---

1. Swift, "Newtown Warehouse."

having local contacts helping to ensure that whatever they did was beneficial.

A second issue that Jennifer needed to sort through is what counts as ministry or service. Teaching English to adults seems less fulfilling than hugging a poor child in an orphanage. But again, the question is not how we feel, but how well our efforts are integrated into a larger effort to love and serve people in a particular community while connecting them to ongoing, local resources. This is where partnership with local churches or other agencies is so important! Additionally, we must be aware that we all have different gifts and abilities that can be used in diverse ways. The author of 1 Corinthians, speaking about spiritual gifts, notes that such diversity is good. "There are different kinds of gifts, but the same Spirit distributes them. There are different kinds of service, but the same Lord. There are different kinds of working, but in all of them and in everyone it is the same God at work" (1 Cor 12:4–6, NIV). *Effective ministry makes use of the talents that we have, matched to the needs that exist, within a context of ongoing local ministry.*

OFFERING OUR GIFTS TO GOD

Let's consider the Scripture verses with which this chapter began. The context of the first verse is quite surprising. Paul and Timothy addressed a letter to the church in Colossae, a church they had never visited. Having heard of their conversion, though, Paul and Timothy wanted to encourage the new Christians in Colossae. In the letter, Paul provides theological instruction, especially noting Christ's reconciliation of all things through his incarnation and crucifixion. Paul discusses salvation and encourages young Christians not to submit to errant human rules (however "spiritual" they may sound) but instead to live as those who have been raised with Christ. Therefore, the Colossian Christians are encouraged to avoid evil (sexual immorality, impurity, lust, evil desires, greed, resentment, anger, malice, foul language, and dishonesty) and to clothe themselves in righteousness (compassion, kindness, humility, gentleness, and patience), forgiving and loving one another in the peace of Christ. Paul then turns his attention to relationships: between wives and husbands, between children and parents, and between servants and masters. And so we read, "Whatever you do, work at it with all your heart, as working for the Lord, not for human masters, since you know that you will receive an inheritance from the Lord as a reward" (Col 3:23–23, NIV). While the original context clearly involves slavery (something that was ubiquitous in the ancient world), there is a hint here that everything we do can be done for the glory of God. Christian service is not limited to spiritual things like preaching and running vacation Bible school! Christian service involves any activity which is done "for the Lord."

Likewise, the second biblical passage with which this chapter began included instructions from Paul about diversity within the body of Christ: "We have different gifts, according to the grace given to each of us. If your gift is prophesying, then prophesy in accordance with your faith; if it is serving, then serve; if it is teaching, then teach; if it is to encourage, then give encouragement; if it is giving, then give generously; if it is to lead, do it diligently; if it is to show mercy, do it cheerfully" (Rom 12:6–8, NIV). Service Learning Teams and short-term mission teams will engage in many different types of ministry, but in all cases we should serve others as an expression of the love of God.

KEEPING A MISSIONAL FOCUS

So, we might reasonably ask, how do we keep a missional focus, whether we are teaching vacation Bible school, engaging in medical missions, or lecturing on an academic topic in a foreign university? As we have already seen, the first prerequisite is often making sure that we are working with local people so that our short-term work reinforces existing long-term ministries and relationships. We must lean on them and defer to their judgment.

Second, we need to keep in mind cultural differences that affect how we carry out service. My friend Jack often travels to developing countries. He will often tell students that the cultures in which they work value relationships more than tasks. If someone comes up to talk to him while he is painting a wall, he just puts the paintbrush down and talks, sometimes for an hour or more. Task-oriented North Americans often want to prioritize the job— get the painting done!—while local people prioritize relationships. You need to minister in culturally competent ways.

Third, we need to prepare for the work. Teams need to pray for each other and for the opportunities they will have. Whether a team is working in an orphanage, teaching English, or holding a medical clinic, solid preparation must take place in the weeks and months before the team departs. The exact preparation will, of course, depend on what the team will be doing (a healthcare team and a choir will obviously need different preparation and require people with vastly diverse skills!). In any case, though, the group must learn to work together. This is one of the reasons regular group meetings, where all the members of the team are present, are essential. In such meetings we can make sure that members know how their service fits into the larger picture, assist in building group cohesion, and ensure that the group is prepared for the tasks they will engage in.

Finally, during the time when the team is engaged in service it can be helpful to have daily group meetings. At the beginning of the day it is helpful to gather for a brief devotional that can form a context for the day ahead. Some leaders prepare devotional readings for the entire period of travel, which they print with a daily itinerary. Others may prefer a more serendipitous approach. The morning meeting should also be used to go over the events planned for the day. At the end of the day, a debriefing session should be held, with ample time to process things such as ways the team sees God at work, things that may pose challenges to faith, an analysis of what is working well, and an honest assessment of where there may be tension points. Team members can close the day in prayer for one another and for those that they have encountered that day.

In recent years I have included the following prayer in the printed itinerary for groups that I lead. I have not been able to discover anything of the origins of the prayer, though it is oddly named the Grail Prayer. I have found it useful for us to recite this prayer together each day as a way of reminding ourselves that whatever we do, we should be offering it as service to God and to others.

> Lord Jesus,
>> I give you my hands to do your work.
>> I give you my feet to go your way.
>> I give you my eyes to see as you do.
>> I give you my tongue to speak your words.
>> I give you my mind that you may think in me.
>> I give you my spirit that you may pray in me.
>> Above all, I give you my heart that you may love in me
>> your Father and all mankind.
>> I give you my whole self that you may grow in me,
>> so that it is you, Lord Jesus,
>> who live and work and pray in me.
>> Amen.

∼

1. Look back at Jennifer's experiences in Central America and the Middle East. Why might she have had a stronger emotional sense that her work in an orphanage was more spiritual or satisfying than her team's work in an English café? What could her team have done differently to make their work in the orphanage more effective?

2. Why do we sometimes feel good when we do things that are actually not helpful, such as sending teddy bears to victims of

mass disasters, or inefficiently collecting donated water that must be transported to a distant place where there is a need for water?

3. How can we make sure that our efforts to help are indeed helpful and not harmful?

4. The author claimed that effective ministry makes use of the talents that we have, matched to the needs that exist, within a context of ongoing local ministry. What talents and abilities do you have that might be useful in the context of the Service Learning Team or short-term mission team that you are considering?

5. How can you keep a missional focus as you prepare for your Service Learning Team or short-term mission team? What kind of preparation do you need to engage in for this experience?

6. How might the Grail Prayer—or something similar to it—be useful in framing how you use your abilities and resources in everyday life and while participating in a Service Learning Team or short-term mission team?

9

Reflections during Service Learning Experiences

They returned from exploring the land after forty days. They went directly to Moses, Aaron, and the entire Israelite community in the Paran desert at Kadesh. They brought back a report to them and to the entire community and showed them the land's fruit. Then they gave their report: "We entered the land to which you sent us. It's actually full of milk and honey, and this is its fruit. There are, however, powerful people who live in the land. The cities have huge fortifications. And we even saw the descendants of the Anakites there. The Amalekites live in the land of the arid southern plain; the Hittites, Jebusites, and Amorites live in the mountains; and the Canaanites live by the sea and along the Jordan."

Now Caleb calmed the people before Moses and said, "We must go up and take possession of it, because we are more than able to do it."

But the men who went up with him said, "We can't go up against the people because they are stronger than we." They started a rumor about the land that they had explored, telling the Israelites,

> "The land that we crossed over to explore is a land that devours its residents. All the people we saw in it are huge men. We saw there the Nephilim (the descendants of Anak come from the Nephilim). We saw ourselves as grasshoppers, and that's how we appeared to them."
>
> —Num 13:25–33, CEB

WHEN MOSES WAS PREPARING to lead the people of Israel into the promised land, he recognized the importance of obtaining firsthand reports. Admittedly, the twelve spies who were sent to Canaan did *not* constitute a Service Learning Team, but we can still learn something from their experience. The spies brought back artifacts—fruit—to demonstrate what the land was like. They gave a descriptive account of its people and its fortifications. So far, the twelve spies seem to be pretty much in agreement. But then, we move to subjective reflections: ten of the men are so terrified that they begin (consciously or unconsciously) to exaggerate the threats that await them, while two other men, Caleb and Joshua, try to reassure the people that God is with them and that they can manage the task of taking the land. Now, while this chapter discusses how to take effective notes and how to best engage in reflection during a Service Learning Team experience, we have to make a side observation here: fear and complaining can spread like wildfire! If you want to have a healthy team experience, do not let yourself fall into bitterness and complaining.

But, back to our main point. Clearly, the spies in this story were not doing sociological research, but they were making observations, both objective and subjective ones. We actually see several places in the Bible where travelers describe the things that they see (cities, temples, geography, and so forth) and experience (positive and negative interactions with others, conversations, tastes of food and wine, and so forth). Their records were often sent by letter so that they could share and reflect on their experiences with others.

(Aha! The blogs we keep of our experiences are simply a new form of a very old practice!)

FIELDNOTES: IMPROVING REFLECTIONS THROUGH DELIBERATE PRACTICE

For academic purposes and to improve the quality and depth of reflection during a Service Learning Team, we encourage students to take careful fieldnotes. So, what are fieldnotes? Fieldnotes are qualitative observations used by social scientists to record and reflect on their experiences. While they do provide a record, they are imperfect—they are affected by biases (whether or not we are aware of them) and by human limitations (memory is not perfect or exhaustive, so we only record a limited amount of what we experience). Of course, different people see things from quite different perspectives.

Objectivity does not come easily. Wherever we go, we take our biases and our fears and our hopes and our dreams with us. Our culture, history, and language shape how we see the world. This is one of the reasons that we encourage participants to take fieldnotes while on a Service Learning Team or while traveling or studying in an area that is foreign. By taking structured notes, we can begin to sort out descriptive information from more subjective reflections which contain our hypotheses about why things are the way they are.

During one Service Learning excursion I was struck by the diversity of my team members' fieldnotes. One person, an art major, wrote somewhat disparagingly about famous Renaissance paintings that we saw in a museum because they were not done in a style that appealed to her. Another person described the appearance and taste of food so vividly that you could almost taste it while reading her descriptions. A third member of the team wrote glowingly about encounters with people, describing clothing, behavior, and mannerisms in great detail. A fourth member took meticulous notes about how people managed their pets; I was amazed to realize that I had never noticed that people in this country did not keep their dogs leashed—they were perfectly trained to walk at their owners' heels and not to chase wild animals or to interact with other dogs or people!

HOW TO TAKE FIELDNOTES

Fieldnotes begin with *descriptive information*—the time, the date, the geography and physical environment, the social environment (including interpersonal interactions and social roles). Your journal might include descriptions of natural features of the environment, of infrastructure or architecture, of the local food or dress, and so forth. Use your senses to describe what you are experiencing: what do you smell, hear, taste, see, and feel as you participate in different experiences? Fieldnotes can also include your own reactions, and you might include sketches or recordings of your experiences. The second component of fieldnotes is *reflective information*. This includes deeper consideration about what you have witnessed and might include theories, questions, ideas, and concerns. Taking fieldnotes can allow you not only to document your experience but to think more deeply about it.

Here are a few general guidelines to assist you in taking good fieldnotes. First of all, you can't possibly observe everything, so decide in advance if there are particular things you want to focus on (e.g., commerce, religion, family relationships), but don't let this keep you from making novel or unexpected observations.

For Descriptive Content

1. Describe the physical setting (geography, architecture, transportation, and so forth).

2. Describe people and their social environment (verbal and nonverbal communication, social interactions, specific events).

3. Record exact quotes or summaries.

4. Describe what you see from your perspective, and what you think might have been taking place from the perspective of the people you observed. Describe any way that you think your presence might have altered the social setting; your presence changes things!

For Reflective Content

1. Record your own impressions, thoughts, and hypotheses about what you observe.
2. Record a list of questions that arose during your reflections. Don't edit these to be "politically correct" or to fit a preconceived theory—let these arise spontaneously and evaluate them later.
3. Reflect on your own perspective. What biases might you be bringing into this situation that might alter your observations and conclusions?
4. Make notes about things that you want to investigate further.
5. Allow the fieldnotes to build on previous entries—you may find that you want to clarify, reject, or strengthen previous observations.

Let me illustrate this process with an actual example. While I was writing this book, my wife and I were helping our oldest daughter look for an apartment in Tennessee. Following are my fieldnotes on the morning of our second day.

A TENNESSEE EXAMPLE OF FIELDNOTES

I've only been here for about fifteen hours, and eight of those were spent trying to sleep. Still, in that short time, there are a lot of cross-cultural observations to be made. Let's start with the physical location. I am sitting in the open concept living room of an Airbnb apartment that we are renting. The downtown area has lots of boarded-up shops. Our second-floor loft apartment is in a seven-story brick building, built in 1912, that used to be a bank. It is now a mixed-use building, with the first floor occupied by businesses, and the other floors have both apartments and business suites. The interior has original brick walls with arched windows, as wide as they are tall. The modern replacement windows, laminate and tile floors, and décor are clear signs of fledgling urban renewal. The owner of our loft has eclectic tastes. There is an exercise machine in front of an arched window, with a red watering can set on the sill as decoration. The large brick-arched framed windows give a trendy chic vibe to the place, but the finishings are inexpensive—the kitchen has economical cabinets and pink Formica countertops and an old dishwasher. The bathroom vanity is cheaply made, and the hot and cold water are plumbed backwards in both the kitchen and the bathroom, making me think they did some of the renovation work themselves. The furniture is mismatched but comfortable. There are no doorways between bedrooms and living space. The second bedroom is in the old bank vault, with the massive vault door standing open and an iron grated gate that can be closed.

There are over half a dozen nicely framed pictures throughout the loft. Some are watercolors that use subdued tones, sometimes accented with a sudden splash of a brighter color. Others are pastel and charcoal sketches. Most are nudes or semi-nudes in which the faces are somewhat obscured. As I looked closer, I noticed that all of the pieces were signed by the same artist, mostly between 2007 and 2009. A watercolor is in the alcove. It is by the same artist, but its style is different, it is a beautiful harbor view with what might be a domed church behind the small moored boats. It reminds me of Venice. Three of the watercolor pieces are unframed rough sketches of the unclothed back, head, or chest of the same man. They are titled Eric, which is the name of one of the owners of the loft. They are dated between August and November of 2012. So, apparently, the owners know this artist.

Last night there were at least three loud freight trains, horns blaring repeatedly at each railroad crossing. The trains may provide some clues about local industry. Another clue was the loud voices

Reflections during Service Learning Experiences

coming from the street below in the wee hours of the morning as people left bars and restaurants. By the light of morning, I can see empty offices in the building across the road. There are lots of empty storefronts and signs advertising space for sale or lease. And then there is a beautiful courtyard fountain. All of these things point to what is a common trend in many cities—an abandoned and deteriorating downtown caused by the flight to the suburbs, but now people are trying to renew the inner city with mixed success.

Dinner last night was full of cultural elements. We ate in a restaurant that was a converted train station. Our waiter, Tucker, spoke in a soft Southern drawl. (I wonder how he would describe my accent.) He was friendly, happy to make recommendations and to joke around with us. He was probably in his early twenties, dark hair, lots of tattoos, with a broad, friendly smile and twinkling eyes. The restaurant was upscale Southern themed—perfect for downtown renewal—with lots of fried foods and Southern side dishes that we just don't have up North. The décor featured a lot of train-themed artwork and seating areas were separated by stained-glass windows and old window frames that had been repurposed as hanging partitions. I briefly thought about ordering the half chicken soaked in sweet tea brine and then grilled. The three of us shared a pecan and brown-sugar–glazed bacon appetizer, biscuits with blueberry jam made in the restaurant, followed by fried chicken salad; fried chicken with gravy, French fries, and grilled brussels sprouts; and a thick pork chop served on top of a corn fritter pancake covered with sassafras sauce and fried pork belly. I've always thought that food is a great way to understand a culture. There is no apologizing for how unhealthy this food is. It's just a celebration of life poured over the taste buds, meant to be shared with good friends.

Why are fried foods so prevalent here? Lots of pork and chicken, not much beef—perhaps lower income or agricultural factors skew the meats in that direction. The soil looks poor from an agricultural point of view, so I'm guessing this might have been an area where the tobacco trade flourished.

While we were out today, I received a text from Eric asking if he could get into the loft because he needed to pick something up. I *told him that was fine, that we were out anyway. When we returned we found a nice note from Eric, with a bottle of champagne and a dozen farm-fresh eggs. It's hard to know how much of this is Southern hospitality and how much it reflects Eric's personality, but the friendliness and helpfulness of people here is definitely a contrast to the characteristic feel of many other parts of the country. People in the grocery store went out of their way to recommend apartment complexes, restaurants, and would happily talk well after the business transaction of buying the groceries was over.*

The area immediately around downtown is fairly flat, but the foothills of the Appalachian Mountains lie just a few miles away. It is stunningly beautiful. The mountains beckon you to come. They call for you to enter their depths. I definitely plan to go hiking on the Appalachian Trail before we leave here. There is a peace and a beauty in these mountains that draw me to awe, wonder, and worship.

I have so many questions about the local people and culture. What drives the local economy? How do most people live? There are churches all around, a few of which had me wondering if there might be snake handling inside (does my question reflect wild tales I've heard about snake-handling churches or are these just shabby buildings deteriorated by poverty and neglect?). Most of the churches seem to be of the more conservative Protestant type, but there was a smattering of Roman Catholic and mainline churches. What historical factors led to the religious makeup of this area? Are religious congregations losing regular attenders here as is happening in so many other parts of the United States?

I've been surprised that the area is so white—and the Confederate flag is displayed high and proud in places. That makes me cringe. We drove past one farm with a Confederate flag, a U.S. flag, and a Christian flag. What to make of that? I have trouble seeing the Confederate flag as anything but a symbol of racism and a remnant of Civil War defiance. I wonder how people down here think about that flag. I suspect that people are divided, but there hasn't been an opportunity to talk about that. Would people even be honest about it? I am, after all, a Yankee and an outsider. I also wonder if the local friendliness is superficial or deep. Does this place allow people to become part of the community, or are outsiders (particularly "Yankees") always kept at a bit of a distance despite the genuine warmth and helpfulness that one finds here? I obviously have a lot to learn!

∽

So, there you have it. These were real notes taken down during a typical time away from home. It's a good idea to get into the practice of doing things like this. Doing so can help you to solidify memories and to form the habit of asking good questions. Perhaps in time you might revisit your notes and be able to identify biases that you didn't see at first. Or you may find that your reflections cause you to engage in conversation with local people or to explore some of your questions with further research. In any case, you are likely to get more out of the experience of visiting other places if you get into the habit of formally recording your observations and pushing yourself to wonder more deeply about the factors that shape the cultures that you encounter.

∽

1. Apparently, from a purely descriptive point of view, all twelve of the spies gave a similar report to Moses and the people of Israel about the land of Canaan. However, ten of the spies appear to have skewed their subjective report in a way that exaggerated the challenges they would face. What might be some of the reasons for their skewed account? What effect did they have on the community? Why might Joshua and Caleb have provided such a different picture from the other ten spies?

2. Why might taking fieldnotes help participants to get more out of Service Learning and short-term mission experiences?

The Service Learning Book

3. As you look at the author's fieldnotes about his time in Tennessee, identify specific *descriptive* and *reflective* elements. What other questions or observations might have been interesting if you had been in the author's situation and taking your own fieldnotes?

4. During some regular activity (going to church, going to class, eating in the college dining commons), imagine that you are from another part of the world. Take notes about the culture that you see.

10

Finishing Well

> By wisdom a house is built,
> and by understanding it is established;
> by knowledge the rooms are filled
> with all precious and pleasant riches.
>
> —Prov 24:3–4, ESV

> The Lord bless you and keep you; the Lord make his face shine on you and be gracious to you; the Lord turn his face toward you and give you peace.
>
> —Num 6:24–26, NIV

THE BIBLE PROVIDES NUMEROUS accounts of people on journeys, but it often tells us little about the process of going home. As we saw in the previous chapter, the book of Joshua tells us about twelve men who returned after having been sent to explore the promised land. They all gave a glowing report of the goodness of the land, but ten of the twelve focused on the powerful forces arrayed against the Israelites, focusing on giants (whether real or imagined) rather than on God's provision (Num 13). When Jesus sent out seventy-two disciples to preach the gospel, they returned in excitement, rejoicing in what God had done through them (Luke 10:17). In the book of Acts we find some of the earliest missionaries returning to Jerusalem, with nary a report about their homecoming: "When Barnabas and Saul had finished their mission, they returned from Jerusalem, taking with them John, also called Mark" (Acts 12:25, NIV). Just how ought we to think about returning home? If we return poorly, we can be like the spies whose report distorts and ruins the narrative with grumbling and negativity. If we return well, we can reflect on our experience wisely, filling our home with memories that are like "precious and pleasant riches" (Prov 24:4, ESV). We can return in ways that bring blessing and peace, or in ways that fail to make the most of the experience, or which can even cause harm.

THREE PHASES OF CHESS

I'm reminded of an old adage about the game of chess. The game has three phases. In the *opening phase* you work to maximize the space you have for your pieces to work in, and you work to develop a strategy to put your pieces in effective positions; this is like trip preparation. In the *middle game* you assess the benefits of your plan; protect your pieces from counterattack; and assess weaknesses, resources, and logical moves. This is not unlike how the team implements its plans "on the ground," adapting to the circumstances as things play out. Now we come to the *endgame*. A mistake here can cost you the game. An unforeseen threat can turn a win into a loss. And sometimes you may have the advantage, but you just can't figure out how to finish, and so you dance around the chessboard without clear objectives.

Needless to say, this last part of the chess game is crucial. Without a good endgame, the results can be less than satisfactory. So how do we end well?

Finishing Well

Imagine that your Service Learning Team experience or short-term mission trip is almost over. This might be your last night in a hostel before an early morning flight home. Perhaps you are waiting in an airport or sitting in a plane. Or maybe you are in a van driving back from New Orleans or in a dorm room at school after a day working in your local community. In any event, there are a few things you should think about, which are not unlike a good endgame to a chess match: Finish well. Prepare for reentry. Develop at least two narratives to share.

Finish Well

Most Service Learning Team and short-term mission experiences are exhausting. Especially if travel across multiple time zones through several airports on multiple planes and going through customs are involved, you're probably tired. This is often a time when people begin to let their guard down. It's easy to become irritable. You're tired. Other people are tired. You just want to meet someone at the airport, go home, get a shower, and crawl into your own bed. And, so much has gone on! You are filled with memories and stories, many of which are only partially processed. You're going to miss some people and some things about this new place that is now part of your life. You'll miss some of the conversations you had with traveling companions.

But you might also be coming back with some regrets or disappointment. Perhaps you wish you had pushed yourself to be more involved in one way or another. You may miss people that even in a short time you have come to care about. You might feel conflicted about having seen poverty or suffering when you are about to return to a materialistic homeland. Then again, you might be coming back seeing that there are parts of American culture that you used to embrace and now question. Why do we use our cars to go even short distances while people in other parts of the world use mass transit or walk?

Prepare for Reentry

If you have been out of the country, you might have experienced some culture shock on the outward journey. You might now be experiencing what is sometimes called *reverse culture shock*. Suddenly you hear only English. You walk into a grocery store and see two dozen kinds of pickles in the condiment aisle, having just been someplace where it's hard for the average person to get beans and rice for the day. Or, if you have been in a country with a rich culture and a long heritage, you might find it odd that your own country has such a short history and lacks the ornate artistic tapestry of the places you have recently enjoyed.

DEVELOP TWO NARRATIVES TO SHARE

So much is bubbling up in your mind. Very soon, people will ask, "How was your trip?" Your mind spins. Trip? This was much more than that! You learned about other people and how they live. You have seen amazing things, things that you're still trying to wrap your head around. You now have a richer view of what God is doing in the world. You could talk for hours about your experience. When some people ask, "How was your trip?" they will want all the details. But some people will really be satisfied with, "Oh, it was great, I had a good time." And still others will want a ninety-second summary. So, first off, don't be surprised or disappointed when some people really don't want details. It may be helpful to develop a short narrative that will allow you to hit the high points for those who want the ninety-second narrative. What did you do? What are a few of your favorite memories and a few observations? After sharing your narrative, you can end with something like, "If you would like to hear more, let's set up a time to talk over coffee when we both have some time."

This leads to the second narrative. Imagine that you have an hour—or two!—to talk to someone who really wants to hear about your experience. You obviously aren't going to write this out, but it might be helpful to sketch an outline of what this might look like.

Finishing Well

WRAPPING IT ALL UP, AND LEAVING IT OPEN-ENDED

Members of Service Learning Teams and short-term mission groups often find that they now share with each other experiences that few others understand. In addition to developing a short and a long narrative to share with people who ask about your experience, you should also strive to keep in touch with members of your team with whom you can continue to process the experience. Ideally, you shouldn't just say goodbye at the airport and go your separate ways. Being able to have intentional or chance encounters with one another may afford you opportunities to continue processing your experiences. If this isn't possible, forming an email thread or social media group might allow you to continue conversations about your experiences and about how God may use them to shape your understanding of God's work in the world and your own calling. Continued reflection is important if Service Learning or short-term missions opportunities are to be transformative experiences, which will be the topic of our final chapter.

∼

QUESTIONS DURING PREPARATION

1. How might the analogy of the three phases of a chess game help you think about what is needed at various points in a Service Learning or short-term experience for it to be maximally effective?

2. At the end of an intensive cross-cultural experience, you will probably be a bit tired and running on empty. How can you finish well as your time with your team comes to an end?

QUESTIONS DURING OR SHORTLY AFTER THE EXCURSION

1. Think back over your participation and identify some of the key memories that you will cherish. What are some things that you would do differently?

2. Do you have any regrets as your time comes to a close? Is there anything you need to do to end well (perhaps apologizing to someone with whom you had a disagreement, for instance, or just letting the people on your team know what you appreciate about each of them)?

3. What are some observations you have about the people and places that you have experienced? What are some positive things you might take with you that could change the way you approach life?

4. In what way has your view of God's work in the world changed during this experience?

5. Ninety-second narrative—What highlights can you hit in just over a minute? You can always end with, "If you would like to hear more, I would be happy to give you the long version!"

6. Outline of an extended narrative—What would you include if you had an hour or two to talk with someone who wanted details?

11

Looking Back

> But you should control yourself at all times. When troubles come, accept them. Do the work of telling the Good News. Do all the duties of a servant of God. My life is being given as an offering to God. The time has come for me to leave this life. I have fought the good fight. I have finished the race. I have kept the faith. Now, a crown is waiting for me. I will get that crown for being right with God. The Lord is the judge who judges rightly, and he will give me the crown on that day. He will give that crown not only to me but to all those who have waited with love for him to come again.
>
> —2 Tim 4:5–8, ICB

THE APOSTLE PAUL WAS an old man, imprisoned, knowing that he would likely be put to death as a martyr for the gospel of Jesus Christ. In one of his last epistles, Paul reflects on his ministry in a letter to Timothy, a younger man who had been his traveling companion and spiritual protégé. The letter is remarkable. Paul does not seem to be full of fear or regret, but he looks forward to finishing the race well, and he anticipates the reward that awaits him. He remains concerned for Timothy and for the task of spreading the good news and defending sound doctrine. Talk about a spiritual role model!

I wonder how Timothy reacted as he read this letter. He probably saw images in his mind of people and places that he and Paul had visited. He no doubt remembered trials and hardships, as well as successes and joyful times. He was, of course, deeply concerned for Paul, and probably heartbroken at his suffering and his likely fate. Paul, though, wanted to turn Timothy's attention to the mantle that he had to pick up. Paul wanted Timothy to be a person of integrity and conviction, spreading the gospel and dedicating himself to serving God and others. So, we are back where we started: in the end, *how do we love our neighbor?*

The impact of having been a member of a Service Learning Team or of a short-term mission team can be quite significant—or it can be just a blip on the radar screen. The difference will largely depend on how deeply you reflect on it and how much you allow it to permeate your own outlook on life. Periodically, in the weeks, months, and years after you return, it may be helpful to look back on the ideals you have explored in this book so you can evaluate how you are doing at following God's call on your life.

Service Learning Teams and short-term mission teams are not extensive missionary journeys of the type that Paul and Timothy embarked upon. And they certainly don't have the kinds of hardships that Paul and Timothy experienced. But they can still be marking points that help you to think about your priorities, long after the experience itself is over. You may find that the following questions can be helpful in guiding your reflections at various times—a month, a year, or many years after returning from a Service Learning Team experience.

1. In what ways did your Service Learning Team or short-term mission team experience help you learn to love others better? How can you love others better in your current situation?

2. In retrospect, how can you see God having prepared you for this experience?

3. How has God used your experience in your life since you returned? For instance, have you improved your cross-cultural awareness? Do you have a bigger picture of what God is doing in the world and how you can participate in the redemptive work of the gospel?

4. As you face current decisions, how can you see the signposts that Garry Friesen talked about working in your life now? (Friesen's signposts are the Bible, circumstances—"open and closed doors," the inner witness of the Holy Spirit, mature counsel, personal desires, common sense, and special guidance.) Do you find yourself looking for billboards rather than nudges and wisdom?

5. One of the things that sometimes sabotages Service Learning Teams is a lack of commitment—people who drop out or who don't meet their responsibilities in team preparation. What commitments do you have now? What do you need to do to make sure you are committing to things that are beneficial, and that you are carrying them out? Are you overextended? Do you need to cut back or to find new opportunities to serve God and others?

6. Service Learning Teams and short-term missions are only possible with the support of others. How are you doing with cultivating gratitude for the ways that others have invested in you? How are you doing in generously supporting the work of God and the opportunities that other people have to make a difference in the world?

7. Traveling in close quarters to unfamiliar places while sleep-deprived is a recipe for conflict. What have you learned about your own vulnerabilities to conflict? How are you doing with conflict resolution and forgiveness in your current situation?

8. Cross-cultural encounters allow us to see the world differently and to see the perspectives of others more clearly. How do you see your own culture and country differently as a result of your cross-cultural experiences? How are you doing with continuing to develop cross-cultural competency?

9. Looking back on your time on a Service Learning Team, you've probably realized that it is easy to collect a lot of stuff and to think we need more than we do. How are you doing with this? Do you need to simplify your life or let go of some of your possessions?

10. Looking back on your Service Learning experience, what are you grateful for? What might you do differently? How has this experience shaped you in the time since then?

Hopefully, these questions may—at various points in time—help you to continue processing your experience.

In the Old Testament, people sometimes erected monuments—called *tels*—to remind them of what God had done in a particular place. Perhaps this journal can itself be a *tel* for you as you reflect on your experience. My hope is that your journal—your tel—will confirm the advice that Paul gave to Timothy: "When troubles come, accept them. Do the work of telling the Good News.

Do all the duties of a servant of God" (2 Tim 4:5, ICB). If being on a Service Learning Team or engaging in short-term missions helps you to become better at loving God and loving your neighbor, then all the time and effort involved will have been well worthwhile!

Bibliography

Broadwell, Martin M. (February 20, 1969). "Teaching for Learning." *Gospel Guardian*. http://www.wordsfitlyspoken.org/gospel_guardian/v20/v20n41p1-3a.html/.

Buechner, Frederick. (1989). *The Alphabet of Grace*. 1st HarperCollins paperback ed. San Francisco, CA: HarperSanFrancisco.

Friesen, Garry, with J. Robin Maxson. (1980). *Decision Making and the Will of God*. Portland, OR: Multnomah Press.

Lewis, C. S. (1981). *The Screwtape Letters & Screwtape Proposes a Toast*. Time Reading Program Special Edition. Alexandria, VA: Time Inc.

Nouwen, Henri J. M. (2011). *A Spirituality of Fundraising*. Edited by John S. Mogabgab. Nashville: Upper Room.

Risse, Marielle R. (May 31, 2012). "To Learn Arabic, You Have to Walk the Walk." Commentary. *Chronicle of Higher Education*. https://www.chronicle.com/article/To-Learn-Arabic-You-Have-to/132057/.

Swift, Jennifer. (December 29, 2012). "Newtown Warehouse Scene Shows Why Donations after Sandy Hook Shooting Need to Stop." News. *Litchfield County Times*. http://www.countytimes.com/news/newtown-warehouse-scene-shows-why-donations-after-sandy-hook-shooting/article_d5191fa1-9114-5821-b3cb-20ea094b5f7e.html/.

Additional Resources

SERVICE LEARNING

Astin, Alexander W., Vogelgesang, Lori J., Ikeda, Elaine K., & Yee, Jennifer A. (2000). *How Service Learning Affects Students.* Los Angeles: Higher Education Research Institute, University of California Los Angeles.

Bennett, Claire, Collins, Joseph, Hecksher, Zahara, & Papi-Thornton, Daniela. (2018). *Learning Service: The Essential Guide to Volunteering Abroad.* Wareham, England: Red Press.

Billig, Shelley H., & Waterman, Alan S. (2003). *Studying Service Learning: Innovations in Education Research Methodology.* Mahwah, NJ: Lawrence Erlbaum.

Bringle, R. G., & Hatcher, J. A. (1995). "A Service Learning Curriculum for Faculty." *Michigan Journal of Community Service Learning,* 2(1), 112–22.

Bowman, Nicholas A., Brandenberger, Jay W., Mick, Connie S., & Smedley, Cynthia T. (2010). "Sustained Immersion Courses and Student Orientations to Equality, Justice, and Social Responsibility: The Role of Short-Term Service-Learning." *Michigan Journal of Community Service Learning,* 17(1), 20–32.

Casey, Karen M., Davidson, Georgia, Billig, Shelley H., & Springer, N. C. (Eds.). (2006). *Advancing Knowledge in Service-Learning Research to Transform the Field.* Advances in Service-Learning Research. Greenwich, CT: IAP.

Cress, Christine M. (2013). *Learning through Serving: A Student Guidebook for Service-Learning and Civic Engagement across Academic Disciplines and Cultural Communities.* 2nd ed. Sterling, VA: Stylus.

Darby, Alexa, & Newman, Gabrielle. "Exploring Faculty Members' Motivation and Persistence in Academic Service-learning Pedagogy." (2014) *Journal of Higher Education Outreach and Engagement,* 18(2), 91–119.

De Leon, Nadia. (2014). "Developing Intercultural Competence by Participating in Intensive Intercultural Learning." *Michigan Journal of Community Service Learning,* 21(1), 17–30.

Additional Resources

Driscoll, Amy, Holland, Barbara, Gelmon, Sherril, & Kerrigan, Seanna. (1996). "An Assessment Model for Service-Learning: Comprehensive Case Studies of Impact on Faculty, Students, Community and Institutions." *Michigan Journal of Community Service Learning, 3*(1), 66–71.

Eyler, Janet S. (2000). "What Do We Most Need to Know about the Impact of Service-Learning on Student Learning?" *Michigan Journal of Community Service Learning, 7*, 11–17.

Eyler, Janet, & Giles, Jr., Dwight E. (1999). *Where's the Learning in Service-Learning?* Jossey-Bass Higher and Adult Education Series. San Francisco, CA: Jossey-Bass.

Eyler, Janet S., Giles, Jr., Dwight E., Stenson, Christine M., & Gray, Charlene J. (2001). *At a Glance: What We Know about the Effects of Service-Learning on College Students, Faculty, Institutions, and Communities, 1993–2000.* 3rd ed. Nashville: Vanderbilt University.

Furco, Andrew, & Billig, Shelley H. (2002). *Service Learning: The Essence of the Pedagogy.* Advances in Service-Learning. Greenwich, CT: Information Age.

Jacoby, Barbara. (2015). *Service-Learning Essentials: Questions, Answers, and Lessons Learned.* The Jossey-Bass Higher and Adult Education Series. San Francisco, CA: Jossey-Bass.

Jacoby, Barbara & associates (Eds.). (2003). *Building Partnerships for Service-Learning.* San Francisco, CA: Jossey-Bass.

Kay, Cathryn B. (2010). *The Complete Guide to Service Learning: Proven, Practical Ways to Engage Students in Civic Responsibility, Academic Curriculum, & Social Action.* 3rd ed. Minneapolis, MN: Free Spirit.

Kronick, Robert F., & Cunningham, Robert B. (2013). "Service-Learning: Some Academic and Community Recommendations." *Journal of Higher Education Outreach and Engagement, 17*(3), 139–52.

Mills, S. D. (2012). "The Four Furies: Primary Tensions between Service-Learners and Host Agencies." *Michigan Journal of Community Service Learning, 19*(1), 33–43.

Moely, Barbara E., & Ilustre, Vincent. (2014). "The Impact of Service-Learning Course Characteristics on University Students' Learning Outcomes." *Michigan Journal of Community Service Learning, 21*(1), 5–16.

Pelco, Lynn E., Ball, Christopher T., & Lockeman, Kelly S. (2014). "Student Growth from Service-Learning: A Comparison of First-Generation and Non-First-Generation College Students." *Journal of Higher Education Outreach & Engagement, 18*(2), 49–65.

Root, Susan, Callahan, Jane, & Billig, Shelley. (Eds.). (2005). *Improving Service Learning Practice: Research on Models to Enhance Impacts.* Advances in Service-Learning Research. Greenwich, CT: Information Age.

Simons, Lori, & Cleary Beverly. (2006). "The Influence of Service Learning on Students' Personal and Social Development." *College Teaching, 54*(4), 307–19.

Strait, Jean R., & Lima, Marybeth. (2009). *The Future of Service-Learning: New Solutions for Sustaining and Improving Practice*. Sterling, VA: Stylus.
Tryon, E. A., Stoecker, R., Martin, A., Seblonka, S., Hilgendorf, A., & Nellis, M. (2008). "The Challenge of Short-Term Service-Learning." *Michigan Journal of Community Service Learning*, 14(2), 16–26.
Vogelgesang, Lori J., & Astin, Alexander W. (2000). "Comparing the Effects of Community Service and Service-learning." *Michigan Journal of Community Service Learning*, 7, 25–34.
Ward, Kelly. (2003). *Faculty Service Roles and the Scholarship of Engagement*. ASHE-ERIC Higher Education Report 29/5. San Francisco, CA: Jossey-Bass.
Winston, Fletcher. (2015). "Reflections upon Community Engagement: Service-Learning and Its Effect on Political Participation after College." *Journal of Higher Education Outreach and Engagement*, 19(1), 79–103.
Zlotkowski, Edward, Longo, Nicholas, & Williams, James. (Eds.). (2006). *Students as Colleagues: Expanding the Circle of Service-Learning Leadership*. Providence, RI: Campus Compact.

SHORT-TERM MISSIONS

Backholer, Matthew. (2010). *How to Plan, Prepare and Successfully Complete Your Short-Term Mission: For Volunteers, Churches, Independent, STM Teams and Mission Organisations*. USA: ByFaithMedia.
Corbett, Steve, & Fikkert, Brian. (2012). *When Helping Hurts: How to Alleviate Poverty without Hurting the Poor . . . and Yourself*. Chicago: Moody.
Dearborn, Tim. (2003). *Short-Term Missions Workbook: From Mission Tourists to Global Citizens*. Downers Grove, IL: InterVarsity.
Hempfling, Jack. (2009). *Before You Go: Forty Days of Preparation for a Short-Term Mission; a Daily Devotional*. Maitland, FL: Xulon.
Knaak, Patric. *On Mission: Devotions for Your Short-Term Trip*. Greensboro, NC: New Growth, 2015.
Livermore, David A. (2013). *Serving with Eyes Wide Open: Doing Short-Term Missions with Cultural Intelligence*. Grand Rapids, MI: Baker.
Lupton, Robert D. (2011). *Toxic Charity: How Churches and Charities Hurt Those They Help (and How to Reverse It)*. New York: HarperOne.
Priest, Robert J. (Ed.). (2008) *Effective Engagement in Short-Term Missions: Doing it Right!* Evangelical Missiological Society Series 16. Pasadena, CA: William Carey Library.

FUNDRAISING

Martin, Rob. (2019). *When Money Goes on Mission: Fundraising and Giving in the 21st Century*. Chicago: Moody Press.

Additional Resources

Nouwen, Henri J. M. (2011). *A Spirituality of Fundraising*. Edited by John S. Mogabgab. Nashville, TN: Upper Room.

www.ingramcontent.com/pod-product-compliance
Lightning Source LLC
Chambersburg PA
CBHW020855160426
43192CB00007B/943